THE
CONCATENATOR

THE
CONCATENATOR

A JOURNEY THROUGH HUMAN DEVELOPMENT

CARLO VAN VLIET

MMXVI
ARMCHAIR ADVENTURE
BODEGRAVEN, THE NETHERLANDS

The Concatenator / Carlo van Vliet. - Bodegraven : Armchair Adventure, 2016.
- 172 p. : ill. ; 23 cm. - (Armchair Adventure Publication ; 8).
English translation by N. H. van der Ham.
Cover: John William Waterhouse: The Crystal Ball, 1902.
Copyright for the reproduction of the cover image via Wikimedia Commons
license.
ISBN 978-90-825194-7-1
Keywords: culture studies, universal history, philosophy, psychology
First edition, 2016

Available online via lulu.com
www.armchair-adventure.com
www.concatenator.net

Contents

PART I

ETERNITY

Introduction

To introduce the subject of this book, we will start by briefly indicating what the term 'concatenate' means. A quick look into a random dictionary results in one of the following descriptions: 'to connect to each other', 'to link together in a series or chain', 'subjects that are dependent upon each other'. These descriptions give a general idea of what the Concatenator entails.

Apart from it's definition, the Concatenator is a way to look at the world around us, and to study the ways in which we behave in this world. By using an analytical approach, we will attempt to find out which processes influence the world in which we live. This analysis does not have the intention of stressing or ignoring certain political, religious, social or cultural systems or viewpoints. Nor does it try to wilfully arrange everything into one explanatory system, to, as it were, sketch an all encompassing theory. On the contrary, this analysis rather provides the possibility to go beyond the established '-isms' and provides a way to explain the origin of these systems in particular, and history in general.

By providing an objective and analytical description of the underlying processes of these systems, it will also become clear that the whole structure of the Concatenator is universally applicable. Therefore, the Concatenator doesn't provide an opinion about a certain subject, as it would then lose its relevance. It is much more interesting to get to an objective description of the processes and forces that influence them. Besides, it is evident that these processes in reality have no interest in human opinion. These processes are described at a general level. Readers who would like to gain more in-depth information may make use of the references at the back of this book, or visit the website of the Concatenator.

We will analyse these processes in three parts. First, we will be dealing with the building blocks, the basic principles of the Concatenator. In part two we will focus on man and his relationship with the world from a historical point of view to attempt to explain the ways man has acted in social, political, and religious contexts. And finally we will describe the core of human existence, as dealt with in part one, but then in more detail and from a different point of view.

1 The One Self

Man is an inquisitive being. During our lifetime we walk the earth's surface and, from time to time, we may ask ourselves how the world around us came into being. The question disquiets us. We cannot sit back idly and simply let this matter pass by. We want to study and to discover, in order to increase our knowledge and understanding about life and the world in which we live. To cite the German philosopher Schopenhauer: 'We take no pleasure in existence except when we are striving after something.'[1] And when we wish to develop ourselves as humans, we will want to strive for maturity in different areas, as the Roman philosopher Cicero stated it: 'Not to know what happened before you were born is to be a child forever.'[2] Besides gaining knowledge, every living organism must respond to its environment in order to survive. In doing so, the organism also discovers new things to take advantage of. For many centuries, man has been busy gathering enough information to shape his world, and this has not always been an easy task. This discovery voyage will now be continued by linking together as much of this information as possible, in other words, by concatenating it.

1.1 Everything has a source

Looking at the world around us, sooner or later we will ask ourselves: what is the origin of everything we see? We can do this right now. Perhaps there's a coffee cup or a book, a landscape or another person nearby. What is their origin? We can, of course, give the obvious answers. The coffee cup and the book are man-made. The landscape is formed by the earth. And the other person is the offspring of his or her parents. But these answers can become unsatisfying, at least in the long run. We can of course further specify the answers. The coffee cup and the book are the products of different industrial processes which were developed by man over time. The landscape was shaped by various geophysical processes, which took millions of years to evolve. And the other person is the result of a biological process, in which two opposite sexes of human being mate, resulting in the birth of a new person. These descriptions are more precise, but still not quite sufficient. How did the industrial processes develop? Which knowledge was necessary for it? Can we optimise these processes in the future? Which forces have led to the formation of the landscape? Can we also measure these geophysical processes? Can these measurements provide us with enough information, so that we can map future developments, such as earthquakes? And why do people look the way they do? How do people function? Why does a baby look like his parents, and yet is not an exact likeness?

We could go on endlessly asking questions in this way. There is, however, one important aspect that keeps returning in this process. By asking a new question after every given answer, we become more specific, we go into further details. This will be apparent when we take up the example of the coffee cup once more. Previously, we asked ourselves how the coffee cup was made; the answer was: by man. Then we asked the same question again. This time the more specific answer was: the coffee cup was produced by different industrial processes, that were in time developed by man. Now the next question could be: what kinds of characteristics does the material have? Is it soft or hard? What is the maximum temperature that the cup can handle before it bursts? Is it waterproof? We can continue asking questions in this way until they become very specific, for instance: how are the atoms arranged in the cup? The process with which we can map the world in ever more detail has been going on for centuries, and it has especially been accelerated by the scientific revolution. As the Greek philosopher Anaxagoras said: 'There exists no minimal part of the small; there is always something smaller; and there is always something larger than the large.'[3] The only thing needed is a microscope to map the smallest building blocks, the atoms, or a telescope to chart the map of the immeasurable starry universe, with its giant planets. But for now, we begin close to home, no space travels just yet.

As soon as we examine our own origin intently, we actually also look at the origin of our parents, and their parents etc. In fact, we are looking at the genealogical tree of humanity. Eventually we could end up with a religious creation, or descend every rung of the evolutionary ladder, or maybe we might end up with a combination of the two, or something completely different. For the moment we will put this decision, this belief or gained insight to rest. What we are actually, objectively, interested in, is the core of our being which lies at the base of every human being. What could be the source of it?

Through the mist, above the silence
that sparkle touches
Where thoughts linger, ideas are born
I came crying out

Onwards a million years
what is the core?
Peel yourself off
what is at your core?

When we take a quiet moment to sit and analyse ourselves by mentally slowly peeling away layer after layer, asking ourselves what would be the most important thing in human life? What lies beyond our daily activities and worries, our subjective preferences and rejections, our personal histories and futures, the love or the suspicion that we feel, and perhaps even show to other people? What lies deep beneath the outer layer? What is it that we absolutely cannot live without? What is the core of our existence, of The One Self, besides the society in which we live, our cultural backgrounds, our upbringing or the religion we dedicate ourselves to? Could it be love, family, health, happiness, money, a career, religion or self-preservation? Let's consider these concepts for a moment, and perhaps some others as well, before we tackling them in further discussion.

Love?
Certainly this is very important for the people who are dearest to us. Love is the highest form of trust between people. But is love necessary at any time of day?

Family?
It is often said, that the birth of a child is the most beautiful moment in the parents' life. This is of course seen from their point of view. Actually, the child itself contains his own core.

Health?
Good physical and mental health is indeed important. But there is something preceding this.

Happiness?
A positive approach and experience of life is a good general attitude. But, happiness is perhaps just as often present as unhappiness. Feelings of happiness are pleasant, but they don't belong to our core.

Money?
Can we seriously consider that money is the most important thing in our lives? It does make life easier, it makes most material things more accessible, but it also makes sure that we focus on the wrong things in life, as this line of thought can be seen as too materialistic.

A career?
A successful career gives us a certain social status, and perhaps even personal satisfaction. But is this relevant for a child in an underdeveloped country, who will benefit far more from clean drinking water?

Religion?
For religious people, this is of course an important matter. Religion can give a foothold to cope in difficult times. But, people who aren't religious also have a core.

Self-preservation?
If we are left to solely depend on ourselves, if we can no longer depend upon anyone else, if money, a career, religion etc. no longer matter, then we can only fall back on one important instinct, the instinct of self-preservation, which is the will to survive. All living organisms on this earth must respond and adapt to the world around them in order to stay alive. *In extremis* this means that there is an absolute necessity for The One Self to be able to get out of a life-threatening situation, because existence has the highest priority. Survival is the most basic need, and lies at the very core of every living creature. Self-preservation ensures the continuity of The One Self.
From a human point of view, self-preservation is not the same as being selfish, which is of course rather an anti-social attitude. Self-preservation lies at the base of our humanity, it is our will to survive. It is the preservation of The One Self, apart from the social context. Self-preservation lies at the core of The One Self and applies to every living organism, also to every human, in every situation. Therefore, The One Self is permanently watchful of the environment, wary of possible threats. Is this a safe situation or not? Is this person to be trusted or not?[4] Self-preservation is nature's first law.[5-7]

1.2 What influences The One Self?

Now that we understand that The One Self is the core of human activity, we can continue the analysis. A number of questions we could ask ourselves is: what influences The One Self? What influences self-preservation? What moves The One Self?

We can view the questions again: is it love, family, health, happiness, fear, power, religion, evilness? As before, we can sit down quietly and think these concepts over first before we continue. Bear in mind here that there is one general positive and one general negative force that try to affect The One Self. Let's have another look at the above mentioned concepts. Our description will be based on the generally applied meanings of these concepts, and will not be viewed from a personal standpoint.

Evilness?
Positive: Evilness as a positive force on The One Self? No, that must be a mistake.
Negative: It must be clear that this is indeed a negative force. But, evilness has another source.

Love?
Positive: Yes, this is very important for the people close to us. But it isn't the most important positive force to influence The One Self.
Negative: Love as a negative force? No, the goodness among people is very important.

Family?
Positive: Our next of kin are very important to us, but they are not the most important positive force. For, we mustn't exclude the possibility that someone has no family left.
Negative: No, our next of kin are not necessarily a negative force, unless our family ties are not so good. But this is not what concerns us here.

Health?
Positive: Yes, good physical and mental health are important. But it still isn't the positive force that we are looking for.
Negative: If we should see health as a negative force, then we must be thinking in terms of self-destruction.

Religion?
Positive: Religion can have a central and positive role in people's lives, but it still isn't the general force we are looking for.
Negative: People can have a negative experience with religion, or they can be non-religious. This, however, isn't the most negative force working on The One Self.

Happiness?
Positive: A happy feeling is clearly something positive, but yet again it isn't the most important influence on The One Self.
Negative: Of course we can feel unhappy or depressed, but this feeling or situation can pass.

Power and fear?
Let's take a closer look at these two forces.

We can describe power as *the control The One Self has over a certain situation.* Power is a positive force that we would want to maintain as much as possible. The more power we have, the more control we have over the present situation, the more The One Self remains in a positive state, the less our self-preservation is threatened.
When we know what will happen next, when we are completely at ease in the present situation and no one can put us off balance or give us other ideas, then we are in full control. At this moment, power is the central force of The One Self.
Power is *not* a king or president who governs a country like a dictator. This is an example of the negative use of power. This is when we not only wish to control our own situation, but that of others as well, for instance by forcefully suppressing them. As in wars and crime, these are methods to preserve The One Self, although in a cruel and sad way for all those having to succumb to it. Fromm describes this enforced feeling of superiority at the cost of another:

> To be sure, power over people is an expression of superior strength in a purely material sense. If I have the power over another person to kill him, I am "stronger" than he is. But in a psychological sense, the lust for power is not rooted in strength but in weakness. It is the expression of the inability of the individual self to stand alone and live. It is the desperate attempt to gain secondary strength where genuine strength is lacking.[8]

The other force that influences The One Self is fear. We can describe fear as *The One Self losing control over a certain situation*. Fear is a negative force, which we will want to rule out as much as possible. The more fear we have, the less control we have over the current situation. So, the more The One Self finds itself in a negative situation, the more the self-preservation of the individual is threatened. Fear can be damaging and harmful to us.

When we are uncertain about what's going to happen next, when we lose control over the present situation, then, as a consequence, we can become nervous, depressed, anxious, etc. In that moment, fear is the central force of The One Self.

However, fear can also have a positive effect. When The One Self is seriously threatened in its existence, it triggers our alertness, the adrenaline rushes through our body, enabling us to quickly escape a dangerous situation and thus save The One Self from disaster. Fear can be compared with the effect of pain sensation, whereby a nerve sends a signal to the brain telling it to 'solve this problem quickly, before more damage is done'.

Throughout our existence we will discover various methods and use them to change our daily behaviour to gain power. The One Self has a broad array of attitudes at its disposal in order to gain control over a situation. We use humour, arrogance, exuberant joy, bitter remarks, we reward and we punish, we give the wrong information or none at all, we use physical and/or mental violence, we cooperate or we oppose, we threaten or we console, in short we constantly manipulate the situations we are in. These actions or attitudes ensure that our mental state corresponds with the control over the situation, which is the state The One Self feels most comfortable in.

When there is loss of control over a certain situation, fear becomes the major force, the one we wish to avoid as much as possible. This is why The One Self tries to protect itself using a defence mechanism, which in figure 1 is indicated by a shield. This shield appears in many ways, for instance when we stop watching a movie because it frightens us too much. But, the shield can fail. For example, when we blush our true feelings lay bare for everyone to see, and in certain cases these feelings reveal that there is something which makes you feel uncomfortable. When someone grieves and cries, it means that this person is deeply hurt. This person's protective shield is strongly tested, and by consequence anxious thoughts of more misfortune cloud their mind. Anxiety or negative signals always take priority over good news, as they can threaten the existence of The One Self. The human body is set to immediately respond to signals that detect a threatening situation. For example, in a reflex the signal flashes up the spinal cord and the appropriate muscles come into action, instead of first going to the brain to interpret and evaluate the situation.[9] This doesn't just concern our physical actions, our mental condition or our social well-being are also important. This shield ensures that The One Self is least threatened, it's clearly a defence mechanism.

> In general this kind of fear is defensive, in the sense that it is a protection of our self-esteem, of our love and respect for ourselves. We tend to be afraid of any knowledge that could cause us to despise ourselves or to make us feel inferior, weak, worthless, evil, shameful. We protect ourselves and our ideal image of ourselves by repression and similar defences, which are essentially techniques by which we avoid becoming conscious of unpleasant or dangerous truths.[10]

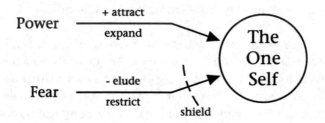

Figure 1: Self-preservation and the forces that influence it.

Now follows an obvious question: why does The One Self not always find itself on the positive side of the influencing forces, where power leads to control over a situation? Unfortunately, this isn't always the case. We simply don't have automatic control over every situation. As we've seen before, a remark made by someone else can make us blush. And this is a relatively harmless example. The country in which we live can become involved in a war, or it can be struck by an epidemic or a natural disaster. Regarding our own lives, we have no say over when and where we were born, who our parents are and the circumstances in which we spend the first years of our lives. Even before we are born, decisions are made about us by our parents. This set of preconditions ensures that, right from the beginning of our lives, we are unique human beings with our own special mix of characteristics. The way we lose control over a situation by an external event becomes clear in the next example.

Let's say we're in a lecture-room, attending a course, and the teacher is giving his lecture below in front of the auditory. We are listening attentively and making notes, when suddenly the side doors down below open and three lions come barging in. The first one attacks the teacher and devours him whole. The second one ascends the left staircase, while the third approaches us from the right staircase. This is a good moment to panic, as we've fully lost control over the situation and we're unsure about what will happen. Especially when the threatening lions are so close, the survival of The One Self is under great pressure.

Of course, in our day-to-day activities we're not confronted with lions entering the room. It's just an example to show how control over a situation can change in a wink of an eye from the positive (power) to the negative (fear). The next example is more realistic.

We're driving our car through the centre of town. Some years ago we got our driving licence, and now, with a few years of experience, we loosely steer at the wheel, while we skilfully manoeuvre the car through the busy town traffic. Suddenly, from a narrow street on the right, a car comes speeding right at us. We try to avoid it, but at the same time we brace ourselves for the crash that's bound to follow. In one moment the power that gives control over the present situation is changed into uncertainty and fear about what will happen next.

As far as behavioural instincts are concerned many things happen automatically. For instance, when you blush, it's unstoppable (even if you're aware of it, trying to stop it only makes it worse). Also, we breathe automatically, and when suddenly something happens our body responds with a startle, something which we have no control over. The autonomous nerve system manages these basic tasks for us, which in this case is all the better. These are bodily responses which we generally needn't think about. Should I run away from the lion entering the lecture-room? Or will I stay and hope that the lion will change his mind suddenly having lost his appetite? Because the basic behavioural responses are so close to the core of The One Self, they have a direct influence on its existence.[11]

Having control over a situation isn't just dealing with a primal survival instinct. We also try gaining and maintaining it in our daily activities. This concerns, for instance, the choice of interior decoration of our homes, our friends, or the type of work that we do etc. In the end though, we need to feel good in our present situation, we want to feel at ease and have control over it. Our permanent drive for control pushes us to the maximum of our capabilities. But, at times things can go wrong, and then we don't realise our role in the world as it is. As a result our self-image doesn't match up with reality.

> Psychologists discovered that a major cause of irrationality revolves around a curious phenomenon known as the 'egocentric bias.' Nearly all of us have fragile egos and use various techniques to protect ourselves from the harsh reality of the outside world. We are highly skilled at convincing ourselves that we are responsible for the success in our lives, but equally good at blaming failures on other people. We fool ourselves into believing that we are unique, posses above average abilities and skills, and are likely to experience more than our fair share of good fortune in the future. [...] For the most part, this egotism is good for you. It makes you feel positive about yourself, motivates you to get up in the morning, helps you deal with the slings and arrows of outrageous fortune, and persuades you to carry on when the going gets tough. For example, research has shown that people are unrealistically optimistic about both their personality and abilities. 94 per cent of people think that they have an above average sense of humour, 80 per cent of drivers say that they are more skilled than the average driver (remarkably, this is even true of those that are in hospital because they have been involved in a road accident), and 75 per cent of business people see themselves as more ethical than the average businessman.[12]

Power and fear are the two forces that affect the core of self-preservation. But often their appearance differs from what we are prone first to expect. Power can disguise itself as hope and longing. When we see power as having control over the present situation, then hope and longing express a desirable situation aimed at the future. The hope or longing for a safe haven in difficult times, for a loved one, or the chance for a new job, ensure that, if this desire is fulfilled, The One Self maintains control or even expands its reach, resulting in a positive situation. But when hope is lost and longing is left unrewarded, the desire to control the situation is not fulfilled. The One Self is then filled with frustration, disbelief or another associated emotion based on fear. Control over the situation is lost and will result in negative feelings. Some time will pass before balance is regained, but eventually new hope or longing will arise, and the entire process will start again.

Although The One Self always strives for as much control as possible to strengthen the degree of self-preservation, and thereby self-affirmation, it can't fully protect itself against external influences. This is especially the case when The One Self disappears, meaning, when our life has ended.

In the domain of philosophy or religion, power is most often based on knowledge and wisdom, which eventually lead to eternal life. Fear, on the other hand, is based on not following or not knowing certain rules, which lead to ruthless suffocation in the fires of hell, or another gruesome place. When one submits or succumbs to the dictated power, dies in a heroic way, or gains access to the deepest insights, then the reward will be respectively a glorious afterlife, eternal goodness and prosperity, or an escape from the cycle of reincarnation. But if one doesn't meet the requirements, then nothing but pain and suffering await till the end of time, a morbid embrace with all things tangible, thus perishable and doomed to decay.

Having control over a situation casts its shadow ahead, not only in the present tense on earth, but also in the afterlife. If you have no control over your thoughts and actions, the only thing that remains is the fear of torture and suffering to eternity.

1.3 Types of The One Self

We've now discussed The One Self, and the forces that influence it. The next step in this process is to find out what the effects are on human behaviour. Every time we engage in a social context, we influence this context or we are influenced by the environment or other people. Even if we aren't present at a specific location and at a specific time, we have indirect influence on the situation or on other people.

There are a number of aspects that stand out when we analyse our own behaviour and that of our fellow man. Figure 2 shows three distinct types of behaviour that can generally be distinguished from empirical and theoretical analysis.

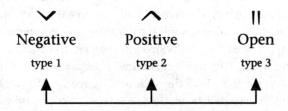

Figure 2: Types of behaviour.

The characteristics of these three types of behaviour can be embodied in three types of individuals, which are described as follows.

The type 1 individual is someone who worries about many things. This individual's self-confidence isn't very high, causing him to often show submissive or humble behaviour. He has difficulty in making important decisions and avoids situations of conflict as much as possible. This person is less sociable and lacking in communication with other people in general. Mostly this type of person will be on his own, as being alone is the situation in which this type of individual feels most comfortable. He tends to have negative, sometimes even depressive thoughts. Because of his repulsion towards the outside world and his negative personal characteristics, the type 1 individual often makes use of negating words in communication, such as 'not', 'never', 'none' etc. Type 1 individuals are soloists.

The type 2 individual is someone who takes initiative. This type of person is an optimist and at times even an opportunist, because he thinks that everything is possible, when by persistence, more than once this individual gets things done. This type of person is spontaneous, is open in communication, and loves taking initiative. He thinks in terms of taking action, rather than acting upon reasoning. This individual has a quick opinion on current news items, likes taking the lead in conversation and activity, and quickly feels at home in every social context. The positive type is someone who believes in himself (e.g. in business or personal goals) or in other things (e.g. a new management theory, the latest hype etc.) and sees potential in them. Because this type has an eagerness to act in this world, individuals of this category often use positive word associations in communication, like: let's do it, we'll take care of it, go for it, let's make it happen, etc.
Type 2 individuals most like being in a group.

The type 3 individual is someone who stands somewhat aside of these former two types, because this type views situations from a distance. Individuals of type 3 are sometimes pulled towards the negative type and sometimes towards the positive type. The type 3 individuals know that the other two types exist, and reflect on them. This type experiences a deeper consciousness of being and has a deeper insight into the surrounding world. This individual isn't interested in the materialistic world and doesn't take position in a pro and contra issue. This type searches for mental balance through contemplation or meditation and is critical about himself and about global issues. Through this balanced look on the world type 3 individuals more often use deliberate words in communication, such as 'when we look at it more closely', 'let's not jump to conclusions', 'you should view all aspects of it', etc.

Type 3 individuals are soloists.

The following examples illustrate how these three types respond differently to the same situation.

A bottle contains a potable liquid. The negative type 1 would say: this bottle is half empty. The positive type 2 would say: the bottle is half full. The open type 3 would say something like: it depends whether you're thirsty or not.

Another example. You're packing your luggage while preparing for a journey. In this situation type 1 individuals ask themselves if everything will go according to plan, more than once go through the luggage to see if nothing is forgotten, and will check several times when to depart. Type 2 individuals already look forward to the moment they arrive at the destination, and can't wait to leave. Type 3 individuals already enjoy the trip while travelling, knowing that the success of the journey doesn't depend on the destination, but on the journey as a whole.

The third example is a bit more abstract. Let's picture a river that represents your total personality, emotions, relationships, history etc. Type 1 will only pick out the negative aspects, and maybe even turn around and walk away from the river. Type 2 will run to the river and jump right in, and will want to drink from it as much as possible right away. Type 3 will sit on the riverbank and observe the streaming water, not tempted to be swept away by the stream of negative and positive thoughts and emotions.

These examples illustrate that type 1 will always provide an excuse not to participate, type 2 will always look forward to the next step and type 3 will evaluate the situation, taking it for what it is.

There is yet another way of looking at these typifications. Type 1 would say 'I hope so' (distancing themselves from the situation, trying not to actively intervene), type 2 would say 'I'll do it' (taking action, being motivated to use the situation to their own advantage), type 3 would say 'I know' (observing the situation cautiously, having no desire to participate).

We can also connect these types of behaviour to the respective forces that affect The One Self. An individual showing type 1 behaviour has less or no control over the present situation and generally has a negative attitude towards life; fear is his most important driving force. An individual of the type 2 nature strives for complete control over the present situation and has a positive attitude towards life; power is his most important driving force. A type 3 individual places himself outside these two influences and isn't as concerned about the forces of power and fear that may impact on this type.

Of course, human behaviour never is as simple or straightforward as presented in the previous examples. It is no given fact that a person under the same circumstances will show the exact same behaviour, every single time. Someone's temper is but one variable that can lead to very different behaviour.[13, 14] Which behaviour an individual shows doesn't just depend on the specific, present situation, but also on things like age, personality, environment, upbringing, intelligence, social background, etc.[15]

Therefore it isn't right to conclude that a person would remain anchored in one of the three defined types of behaviour. For the main part of our lives we can resort to one specific basic type, which represents our behaviour. But it is definitely possible to change to another type of behaviour, which is indicated in figure 2 by three arrows. This behavioural change can take place in the course of a second, an hour or a day, to a few months or perhaps even a few years. Once nestled into the new type of behaviour, the period of time in which one remains there can also be a second, a day, a few months or years, during which time changes to the other two types of behaviour may take place over a shorter or longer period of time.

To illustrate this we can use the earlier mentioned personal mood. From one moment to the next, our state of mind can change from sad (for instance because it's bad weather, or we forgot our keys) to happy (we won the jackpot in the lottery or our partner said 'yes' to our marriage proposal). Unimportant events can have little effect and be short termed. Events with more impact can lead us to change to another type of behaviour for a longer period of time, or even for the rest of our lives.

The total of behavioural expressions a person can show can't be traced back to one single type. The behaviour of a type 2 individual will never completely correspond with all the characteristics of the type 2 description; at certain times elements of type 1 or type 3 will always be traceable in that individual's behaviour.

Taking another look at these three types of behaviour, it should be clear that type 1 isn't ideal for The One Self. Consequently a logical question arises: why does The One Self not always strive for the behaviour of types 2 or 3? The desire for another type of behaviour may actually be present, but a person's behaviour doesn't change as quickly and easily. This is mainly because their present behaviour is based on behaviour displayed in the past. For continuity's sake, the repeated affirmation of a certain action or thought is very important for this individual to be able to justify his own behaviour. It's most reassuring to this person, it's safe, it's familiar territory. In this way The One Self has the most control over a situation and doesn't feel threatened. The constant affirmation of certain behaviour leaves its traces after a while, defining the person, by which we can finally identify this behaviour as a part of someone's personality or character. Even if a person remains under negative conditions for a longer period of time, there may be a need to maintain this situation. It may be a miserable situation, but it is a dependable one. The negative feelings are well known to this individual, so there's no need to switch to another type of behaviour, as this would only produce insecurity, at least in the beginning.

Moreover, much of our behaviour runs on automatic pilot, as it should. Because, if we were to deliberate each and every action we would be getting nowhere. The continuity of behaviour lies at the base of the majority of our actions and thoughts in daily life.

> Out of all the information that our senses pick up, we are only aware of a small part. But this conscious part is not what governs our behaviour. Our behaviour, at least for the most part, is directed by channels that are concerned with other things than creating conscious perception. To these channels it's about efficiency, accuracy and above all the quick switch of sensorial input to motor response. Not words, but deeds. [...] Apparently, in each of us there is a system that determines our actions, without us being aware of the information needed to get there. We do things, without perceiving, and without knowing why, as if we're on automatic pilot.[16]

Most of our actions are taken on automatic pilot, the forces of habit are stronger than the power of will. We can do nothing about it, it's our *modus operandi*. For example, most often we drive our car to town via the same route. We're familiar with this route, we know exactly where we are, the buildings and streets are trusted beacons in the town's infrastructural maze. The landmarks we drive by we use as anchors, they give us control over the situation. But there are so many more, and other roads that lead into town. Why not try taking another route? We'll see a different side of town, which might be prettier or even provide us with a more quiet route with less traffic. But, this requires changing our daily routine, changing our behaviour.

This choice will cost us extra energy to -literally- find the right way, which eventually might lead us to taking the long way round to our destination. Thinking about it, this choice only presents us with a lot of uncertainty. So we decide not to do it. But sometimes we are forced into such a situation. For instance, when there's a road block we'll have to take another route. At such a moment, the uncertainty increases for the exact reason why we don't take another route every day, because we keep losing control. We're unacquainted with this part of town and we're at the mercy of adequate road signs that function as a life line, and we hope for a happy ending. The streets and buildings in this unfamiliar neighbourhood are not our trusted landmarks. Well, don't we ever do something else? Aren't we capable of developing any other behaviour at all? Certainly we do. We learn new things every day, we gather more experience, we become wiser every year. And still, we hardly change our behaviour. We change our behaviour on details, but actually never on the whole. Our increase in experience and knowledge seems disproportionate to changing our way of life. We probably all know from our own experience how difficult it is to change certain behaviour, even if we get better in the long run (understanding the word 'better' here as in better behaviour for ourselves and our surroundings), and yet, we often choose not to change our behaviour. Probably because the short term satisfaction is clear to us, and the long term is simply out of view.

It also deals with the fact that, when we really want to change, we need to experience a moment of self-reflection, asking ourselves: why am I actually doing this? Why do I show this behaviour? Is it wise to keep on doing this? Subsequently we look at the alternatives, wondering 'what else should I do?', where there's always the chance of falling back into the old behaviour and thinking 'why would the new behaviour be better than the old?' Following the 'better alternative', we must put time and effort into it, and perhaps acquire more information. After that, we need to keep repeating the new behaviour, so that the old behaviour is 'overwritten' and the new behaviour becomes automated. Finally, we need confirmation that the new situation is 'better' or 'more responsible' than the old one. In these circumstances it always helps to stick to a certain goal, as for instance with 'if I'd save a certain amount every month, I'd be able to buy what I'd like by the end of the year'. It also helps when the social environment can exert pressure on the intended promise, and can remind us of it at times when we threaten to fall back into our old behaviour. By committing ourselves to a rehab group the pressure and control become even greater. This so-called 'peer pressure' makes sure that the individual behaviour conforms to the behaviour the group requires.[17]

> If you want to change a habit, you must find an alternative routine, and your odds of success go up dramatically when you commit to changing as part of a group. Belief is essential, and it grows out of a communal experience, even if that community is only as large as two people.[18]

A comical look on changing behaviour, or rather on not changing behaviour, is given by Elster:

> A selfish person would refuse an "altruism pill" and, even more compellingly, an altruistic person a "selfishness pill."[19]

From this point of view, we can draw the line further and propose that in many situations people aren't really autonomous, free and conscious beings. Although the human behaviour may establish itself through fixed patterns, functioning almost on automatic pilot, it would go too far to consider humans to be robots. We're always free to change our behaviour, but it's just -as outlined above- that we hardly do it.
In part three the three types of behaviour will be explained further.

At the end of this chapter we've got a starting point. This is The One Self, the core of our existence. We can illustrate it with a dot, a small circle that we will concatenate further.

●

2 The Antagonists

In the last chapter we saw that the state or frame of mind of The One Self is influenced by power or fear, by control over the present situation or the lack of it. These two forces stand, as antagonists, closest to the core of The One Self. We can describe the antagonist as a complimentary force, the opposite of another force, component or element. Let's look at an example from within anatomy. When we lift up our upper arm, muscles in the arm itself, in the shoulder and in the back are needed to flex themselves. To drop the arm, yet other muscles are needed to perform the opposite movement. These muscles are an absolute necessity. If these counteracting muscles were not there, the arm would not be able to go up and down. We'd for evermore be walking about with our arm in an upright position.

As becomes clear from this example, antagonists are elements that oppose each other in function, meaning, etc. They need to, because an antagonist is per definition a contrary element, and there will always be a complimentary contrary element to establish the opposite. This duo, this pair of opposites, forms a steady dual antagonism.

---

left we go
right we go
let the forces push and pull
we attract and reject
balancing, never tipping over
the middle is the mirror

Many of the words, ideas or objects in our environment can be grouped as pairs of antagonists. This counter positioning of words or ideas has already been established in ancient thought, for instance by the Greek philosophers

Pythagoras[20] and Heraclitus.[21] They described the world as a continuing process of opposing sets. The list below shows a number of antagonists to illustrate this concept:

Light	Dark
Left	Right
Male	Female
Plus	Minus
Even	Uneven
Straight	Crooked
Up	Down
Good	Bad
One	Many
Ebb	Flow
Static	Dynamic
Limited	Unlimited
Pride	Shame
Mater	Anti-mater
Order	Chaos
Power	Fear

It appears from this list that all kinds of antagonistic sets can be formed on the basis of polarity which exists in words, ideas, material or immaterial matters, factual data, emotions etc. These sets exist exactly *because* they are their opposites. Is it possible for them to exist separately, not as pairs? Can right exist without left? Can light exist without dark? Can good exist without bad? If everything were to go good or bad, would we still signify or experience it in the same way? Why would we say or think that everything is going well, when it never goes wrong? When the idea or perception of something that goes wrong hasn't occurred for a long time the meaning, the reference to it, simply disappears in daily use. As a consequence, the meaning of good also disappears. Both concepts are necessary, for example, to say something about ethical practice. Antagonists not only are each others opponents, they actually need each other to exist. They attract each other to become pairs, but at the same time they also reject each other because they will never be able to become one. It is important to understand that this is not about the idea of contradicting pairs, in the sense of a conflict. These antagonists rather are two forces that need each other, they form a balanced duality, without which neither would exist. The next description from the Chinese Tao illustrates this:

> The principle of polarity is at the heart of Taoist thought. Yet this emphasis on opposites must not be mistaken for a situation of conflict - everything implies its opposite, and indeed is only meaningful because the opposite is there. And so life and death, light and darkness, good and evil, positive and negative, ebb and flow, and male and female coexist as parts of one and the same system. The elimination of either half would also mean the disappearance of the other.[22]

When we look at the history of humanity, we come across antagonists in various forms in all cultures of the world, such as good and bad behaviour as a basis for ethics in society, day and night as a basis for a calendar. From China we know the pair Yin and Yang, and in Hinduism Shiva is the creator and destroyer combined.[23] We also find the antagonists in the most important moments in our lives: at a wedding or a divorce, at birth or death. During his lifetime every individual will give meaning to these opposing forces.

When we look at The One Self, we also see an interplay of two antagonists, namely power and fear, acting on the concept of self-preservation. They continuously influence the state of mind of The One Self, and, as for controlling the situation, they are as it were the images on each side of a coin.

We can also apply the concept of the antagonists to the three behavioural types from chapter 1. It seems obvious to attribute the negative antagonist to individuals that show type 1 behaviour, and to place the opposing positive antagonist on the side of individuals of type 2 behaviour. But, then there's the third type, the open type, where does this one stand? Actually, type 3 is excluded from the antagonist concept, but this has very much to do with the antagonists themselves. The gathered insight, that belongs to the open type, leads him to understand that prosperity and adversity in life simply cannot be avoided, that these two antagonists are part of everyone's life. Instead of being grabbed by a certain state of mind or by changing circumstances, as occurs to type 1 and 2 individuals in their respective domain, the type 3 individual knows that these complementary pairs are necessary in this earthly existence. Distinguishing and understanding these sets of counterbalanced opposition can lead to greater insight. When we know, that after a negative experience a positive one follows, we understand that everything is balanced. We may then take a different approach to negative and positive events or feelings. We may experience the negative a bit less, and by consequence enjoy the positive even more.

Following these positive and negative characteristics of the antagonists, the starting point at the end of chapter 1 can be seen as a set of counterposed curves, peaking and dipping. The force of the antagonists makes sure that The One Self goes through a positive and a negative phase. In time, through this continuous undulating of forces, a line evolves in the shape of a wave.

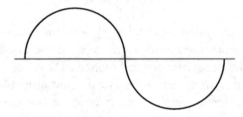

3 Nothing is Lost

In the beginning of chapter 1 we looked at the origin of different objects in this world by repeatedly asking the same question about the specific characteristics of their building blocks. We asked ourselves what could be the origin of a coffee cup, a book, a landscape or another person. This process illustrates that we can always take a step back, there will always be an origin for something to exist here and now. When we continue our questioning like this and delve deeper, we finally end up with something like a religious explanation -a divine entity created the world-, or a scientific explanation -the formation of the universe evolves from the Big Bang-, or some other explanation. We could of course keep on questioning, because, what came before that? The scientist would answer: we just don't know, before the Big Bang there was no time. And the theologians would probably give a similar answer, time only started ticking once the world was created by a divine creature. But can we be satisfied with these answers? Do they actually explain the creation of everything that exists? Basically, this reasoning about the origin of everything goes back in time, until we can't go any further. The answer to our umpteenth question 'but what came before that?' is something like: 'we don't know' or 'nothing'. But then the next question should be: does nothing exist? Can there be nothingness from which something evolves? Do things exist that do not come into being through cause and effect? Can things simply appear out of nowhere? And, no we don't mean the magician who, with his sleight of hand, miraculously makes objects appear or disappear. Here, we all know that we are actually fooled. But we rather mean the 'miracle' of self-generation, that the source evolves from the source itself, without there being a former cause, that this 'nothing' is necessary for 'something' to come into existence. It doesn't get any easier explaining it in this way, because how can we prove that something doesn't exist or didn't exist before?

Let's take a step back for a moment and look at a familiar example from daily practice.

We've just made a nice cup of tea for ourselves, and we've put one sugar lump in it. We could be thinking to ourselves: the sugar is dissolving in the tea. But this is far from true. For, if it were true, the sugar would literally disappear, in other words it would dissolve into the tea. What actually happens is a chemical reaction, namely that the sugar molecules are surrounded by the tea, or rather, by water molecules. The sugar isn't dissolved, but is evenly dispersed in the hot fluid. We *say* that the sugar dissolves, but actually this doesn't happen at all. Apparently our use of words is linked to our visual perception. Evidently the sugar changes from a fixed *form* as grains or a lump into a much smaller fixed form, in which we can no longer detect the sugar as such, as it has seemingly 'dissolved' into the hot water. Then, visually we might be fooled, but we can still engage one of our other tactile senses. When we taste the tea, we can sense that the sugar is actually still there and not simply gone, because the tea has now got a sweet taste.

From this process we can extract the following: nothing is lost, matter transform and disperse differently but remain in existence. In this example the sugar *transforms* from a fixed into a liquid form, but the sugar doesn't disappear. There still is as much sugar as before.

Another example, now from biology. One of earth's natural elements, most important to humans, is oxygen. In biology, the process in which green plants produce oxygen is called carbon assimilation or photosynthesis. By taking in sun light, water and carbon dioxide, a plant produces oxygen and sugar. The sugar is energy for the plant and the oxygen is the plant's waste product. If we write this process down in a chemical formula, there will always be as many water, carbon dioxide, sugar and oxygen molecules in the comparison on both sides of the equal sign, in short: the comparison is balanced. In the process of photosynthesis no atoms are lost, which means that a *transfiguration* of chemical elements takes place in the plant.

The former two examples show that there are various processes that influence matter. We can distinguish three of them. First, the *transportation* of matter, by transporting the water from the tap to the kettle. Second, the *transformation* of matter, by heating the kettle on the stove, resulting in the water going from fluid to gas. Third, the *transfiguration* of matter, by which the decomposition or (re)combination of materials or elements takes place. By leading an electric current through water, the water molecules are separated into single oxygen and hydrogen atoms. The water molecule itself then no longer exists, its identity has been transfigured into two other, newly formed, elements.

These three types of processes are of course dependent on the materials used, the conditions under which these processes take place, the amount of energy that is needed, etc.

Water, in this example, is a substance that lends itself easily for these three steps. But the same applies to all substances, they can change into a different form through these three processes.

These processes can be written down as formulas. A very important mathematical sign, that can't be missed in chemistry, physics, maths, and other exact sciences, is the equal sign (=). This sign enables science to compare differing entities, values or conditions that are part of a formula. What is stated on the left of the equal sign is equal to that on the right, most likely in a different form or proportion. Without the equal sign the formulas in the exact sciences would not function.

In its most elementary form the equal sign can be brought back to for example: $3+4 = 5+2$. What is on the one side of the equal sign is the same as that on the other side of the equal sign, even though the numbers differ.

However, this doesn't just concern maths. In social life we also learn that two different things can be of the same value to us. As children, for instance, we trade two little sweets for one big one, or one we like more. As adults we don't often make difficult formulas or comparisons in our heads when making choices in daily life. We often decide instinctively, or we have so much experience that we swiftly evaluate the pros and cons of our choices. But the decision is always based on an assessment, in which the equal sign forms the balance in the middle.

In science the formulas are often more complex, as we've seen in the example of the photosynthesis of the plant or the relativity theory of Einstein. Here as well, different entities are equated using a formula. In the relativity theory, energy is equal to mass multiplied by the speed of light squared ($E=mc^2$). Each time two entities are compared, but what stands before the equal sign, isn't always the same as what stands after it. Matter, conditions or entities change into other matter, conditions or entities. This seems straight forward alchemy, but this is how matter can change or how connections between matter are made or broken.

Therefore, matter can be displaced, change form, or even be transfigured into one or more other or new substances. But the two antagonists, on both sides of the equal sign, make sure that the balance is upheld. Nothing is lost. The total of the sum remains the same. The opposite, however, is true as well: nothing can simply be added to it.

---

with every step we take
our feet are drifting apart
tripping over cause and effect
we knew from the start
at the end we shake hands

In the beginning of this chapter we asked ourselves if the continuity of the process of cause and effect is always true, or if we will eventually end up with nothing, and if the first occurrence of something can originate from nothing. Because matter can transform into other matter relative to the time spent or the energy supplied or subtracted, an automatic process of cause and effect is started. However, as nothing can ever be lost or spontaneously added, the origin of a cause is always an effect, which in turn finds its origin in another cause.

When we form an image of the process of cause and effect, we immediately come up with a circle. A circle has no beginning or end, and the line which forms the circle stands at the same distance to the centre, all the way round. When we zoom in on the circle, the line actually exists of tiny dots of ink on the paper. Each of these dots precedes the next dot, but each dot also follows up the former dot. The circle in itself is therefore a large sequence of dots that form a line. There is no beginning or end, and all the dots are spread evenly at the same distance to the centre of the circle. With these characteristics the circle is a perfect shape.

The example of the circle has a long history as the unending figurative representation of cause and effect. In many cultures the circle appears in the arts and in religion where it is often seen as a symbol of balance and perfection. Examples of this are the mandala's from India,[24] the wheel of rebirth from Buddhism,[25] and the symbols of Yin and Yang from China,[26] that as two antagonists melt into one, forming a circle. In nature too, we find the circle in both the small and the large. In an atom, where the electrons circle around the core, and in a solar constellation, where the planets circle around the sun. The atom and the planet, both are circular as well, and by repulsion or attraction, everything that goes around them also covers a circular path. The same cyclic path of cause and effect can be applied to The One Self. Biologically speaking, at the end of our lives we will all disintegrate and change into other matter. To us humans applies as well that we exist of substances that previously had another form, that were part of other materials before. Just as the individual cells in our bodies are renewed, our bodies are completely recycled, which obviously only lasts one human life time.

The shape of the wave, with its peak and dip in the figure at the end of chapter 2, now connects with itself by mirroring the image. The beginnings and the ends meet. Nothing is lost, the antagonists are balanced. The symbol of eternity, signifying the Concatenator, is now complete.

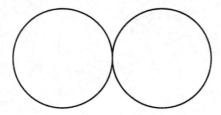

4 Singularity

We began chapter 1 by stating that humans are inquisitive beings, and we are. The first time we open our eyes and can actually see the world, it is 'simply' there. Only when we start asking questions the world becomes incomprehensible. If we want answers to our questions we will have to analyse the world around us. In the history of humanity every civilisation around the world has done so. During early analysis the star constellations were mapped by high priests and medicine men, because they were the earthly contacts between this world and the elusive 'other world'. They explained and gave meaning to the secret symbols and signs. But, in time new questions arose, and at a certain moment this early analysis no longer sufficed. Inquisitive as we human beings are, we went in search of other explanations in answering these questions. This is an ancient quest for the origin of matter, for an understanding of the composition of nature, man's habitat. In India and in Greece some 2500 years ago a theory was formed describing matter as little indivisible spheres.[27] All that we see around us exists out of these so-called atoms. Only recently have we been able to take a picture of this indivisible, rudimentary element, and it actually turns out to be shaped like a sphere.[28] The human quest for explanations, driven by new questions, has led to new discoveries time and time again. Actually, by making these discoveries, we repeatedly go from chaos to order, to chaos, to order, to chaos etc. In the beginning of human history we couldn't explain the world (chaos), so we went in search of answers. The high priests and medicine men found some for us (order). Later came new questions, and the world view then appeared insufficient (chaos), whereupon we went looking for new answers again and created a new world view (order). By constantly raising questions about the world around us, we gain new insights, and in doing so we further specify our view of our surroundings.

> What is this world [...], but a complex, subject to cycles of change, all
> of which show a continual tendency to destruction: a rapid succession
> of beings that appear one by one, flourish and disappear; a merely
> transitory symmetry and a momentary appearance of order.[29]

But, how we look at, analyse and map this world depends on our senses.
We can also try relying on our feelings or our intuition. But this will lead
to a subjective view on the world that differs per individual. If we want to
communicate a structured and united world view to each other, we will need
mutual standards to fall back on. Our senses in this case are the basis for the
perceptions we share with each other and repeatedly put to the test. As mentioned before, man perceived the world in this way in the early analysis. The
sun was the perfect spherical provider of our daily light. The heavens were
full of stars and planets, that yet other celestial bodies circled. The celestial
clockwork gave us low and high tides, day and night, and the seasons every
year. Everything was in perfect symmetry, consisting of cycles of cause and
effect, just as harmoniously perfect as a circle.

But this early analysis of the world view had its limitations. Take for instance
a random insect, which experiences the world around it very differently
from the way we do. To begin with, the insect sees the world from a different
perspective. But, this doesn't just concern visual perception. A dog's sense
of smell, for example, is far better than ours.[30] We have a limited range of
detecting smells, and processing them by our brains. Therefore our view of
the world is dependent on the capacity of our senses, of what we can perceive.
So, we may say, man truly is the measure of all things, that is, from his own
point of view of the world. But, if we are so dependent on our senses, to what
degree is our world view still objective and dependable? When we cannot
see or smell, let alone hear, taste or touch something, does this invariable
mean it doesn't exist?

In human history these questions were repeated in the ensuing sequel of
analyses on the world view. Each time the system concerned (order) has no
viable answer to our questions we go in search of a new system yet to be
discovered (chaos). When we look more specifically, we see that the moon
isn't perfectly round, that the earth's orbit around the sun is rather an ellipse
than a perfect circle, and that a day isn't exactly 24 hours long.

This development in research actually is rather self-evident. The more precise
we can measure, the closer we can get to reality, the more insight or control
we gain over the situation. We can't rely on a very general measure or on
something somebody mentioned, such as 'I thought it was a cold winter',

we want to make it measurable. Only by having done that, we gain an objective independent value. Subsequently, we can determine if this winter was colder or less cold than previous winters. This practice of measuring results doesn't just concern the so-called scientific method, but also information in general. For instance in daily life, when we set a meeting with someone 'somewhere in the afternoon', it will be far more difficult to actually meet, than if we were to set the appointment 'at three o'clock by the entrance of the central station.'

This continuous specification of the world view has these days resulted in building even bigger particle accelerators to find ever smaller components of the atom. And, we're building even bigger telescopes that orbit our planet through which we're trying ever more to look back in time, in search of the first galaxies. We are looking further and further into the universe and it continues to astound us.

---

how to describe the perfect problem?
no apparent reason for cause and effect
chaos conjures up order
logically it's hard to neglect

mixing up back to front is the trend
with the beginning, start the sentence
order conjures up chaos
leaving only question marks at the end?

When we continue to specify our world view, when we continue discovering, and the description and understanding of our world view become ever more detailed, will we be able to uphold our current suppositions?

Do the planets and atoms describe a perfectly round course around a central point, and does the cycle always end up exactly at its beginning? Are there counterparts to every characteristic, do we find antagonists everywhere? Is indeed nothing ever lost, will everything remain in existence, yet in another form? The answer to this is: no. A different situation exists.

In physics this alternative situation is termed a singularity. This is an exceptional situation that is in conflict with all the laws of nature. During a singularity nothing is certain. All the laws of nature that usually apply, don't apply then. Everything that can be calculated, every predictable result based on cause and effect, the balance between antagonists, the balance between the two forces at either end of the equal sign, they all disappear in the state of singularity. The most well-known example of a singularity is the Big Bang theory. The question as to how a singularity works and what happens exactly is difficult to answer, because the natural laws with which we describe our universe don't apply and are unusable in this context. The current view on the Big Bang singularity in science is that of a situation in which the whole universe is concentrated at a single spot. As a result of extreme high pressure and temperature, the Big Bang in effect caused the present universe, which is still expanding.[31] While a singularity breaches with all known laws of nature, thereby being a great unknown, it's not unlikely to envision that everywhere large and small singularities exist or are just developing. Black holes are such an example, a phenomenon in the universe where a burnt up sun implodes and by that absorbs all energy and matter around it, so that nothing escapes. A singularity is actually like a transfiguration, as described in the former chapter, in which all materials change, they disintegrate or rather make new connections. Cause and effect, as they would occur under conditions known to us, have now become useless. All laws of physics are violated, as this is a phase of total chaos.

But then, will this situation continue to exist? The answer to this question is also: no. A singularity devours everything and resets the basic materials of the universe. It's like a complete maintenance overhaul of everything in existence, which of course needn't be the same car driving out of the maintenance garage.

As to the existence of the Big Bang singularity, there actually are just two possibilities: either there has never been a singularity or there has.

In the first case, chaos is not the cause of the emergence of the universe. This would mean that there always was order, that all the laws of nature have always existed. The processes that take place as described in chapter 3 Nothing is Lost, and the attraction and repulsion of matter as described in chapter 2 The Antagonists, all have a place in this.

In the second case, a singularity has taken place. After the emergence of chaos, nothing can happen other than the formation of a new order, with new matter for a new universe. This new order will be based on finding balance. The antagonists will apply the forces of attraction and repulsion. The concept of 'Nothing is lost' will also be of influence. The emergence of life as a human being is a result of this new order. And in turn we have discovered several levels in this order, for instance in the concept of cause and effect. After a while this order can collapse again and pass into the chaotic situation of a new singularity, that on its own transfigures into a new order. And, perhaps there will be a new species, that, with an inquisitive stance like ours, will investigate his environment and try to understand the world. The One Self will perhaps reappear in a known or a whole new form. After this new order, again comes chaos, and the whole process will start again. As such, the universe finds itself in a continuing cycle of attraction and repulsion. It's like a start finish banner at a race, where there is start written on one side and finish on the other.

Regardless of which of the two possibilities is correct, the principles that were described before remain. If all matter was formed once from a single point, or if it repeatedly retracts to one point, this would be equal to the concept of a dot that we placed as a graphical representation at the end of chapter 1. Then the antagonists will again strive for balance. Nothing will be lost, only the spread or shape of matter may be different. The symbol of the Concatenator refers to this ever present, unendingly undulating cycle.

Is this a sufficient answer? Have we returned to the starting point? No, not completely. The Concatenator is, above all an open system, to which new elements can be added. So there is no reason to try to produce a closed circuit of formulation. There are still enough gaps in our knowledge that can be filled with new information in the future. It is also better to acknowledge that certain questions are difficult or impossible to answer at a given moment. It is fruitless to establish and hold onto a closed system, which needs amendment after a while, unnaturally squeezing in necessary changes or additions, so that the system in time becomes an illusive shamble.

In addition, accepting the idea that not everything can presently be explained, also counts as a kind of preliminary solution, if only for the sake of our peace of mind. This resembles the idea that asking the right question already contains half of the answer. We've got lot's more questions, and so much more to discover. Man will remain inquisitive, face new chaos and analyse it to produce a new order. New building blocks await us in the future, so let's continue on our path of concatenating all the information.

> When I see the blind and wretched state of man, when I survey the whole universe in its dumbness and man left to himself with no light, as though lost in this corner of the universe, without knowing who put him there, what he has come to do, what will become of him when he dies, incapable of knowing anything, I am moved to terror, like a man

transported in his sleep to some terrifying desert island, who wakes up quite lost with no means of escape. Then I marvel that so wretched a state does not drive people to despair.[32]

•

PART II

WORLD

Introduction

In part one we looked at the building blocks of human motivation and the world in which we live. In part two the most important processes of social, political and religious developments and that of the individual are outlined against the backdrop of our general history. When we look at the specific characteristics of these processes, we can categorise the way in which man shapes his environment into three phases. These are in succession: the natural, social and communicative phase. In broad outlines, and allowing for local variations, these phases continuously manifest themselves in the social development of all cultures around the globe. The phases define the way a community functions, which political system is applied, whether the people practice a religion and the social consequences of this practice for the people and for the individual as part of that community. The definition of these phases and the boundaries in between are somewhat subjective, but this division into three phases is recognised by various authors.[1-3]

Through study at the end of the 19th century, anthropologists gained the idea that when they engaged into advanced contact with another culture the development of that culture would proceed according to a number of fixed stages.

> Early anthropologists had also been affected by the colonial experi-
> ence: on several occasions attempts were made to educate colonised
> populations, the aim being to convert them to the 'obviously' superior
> European cultural practices. The fact that these attempts had all failed
> persuaded at least some anthropologists that there had to be 'a fixed
> sequence of stages through which all cultures develop'. And it followed
> from this that one could not, artificially, boost one culture from an
> earlier stage to a later one.[4]

Although the transitional boundaries of the different phases are subject to discussion, the transitions are often marked by a revolution. The leaders are thereby forced to give up their power, which is the control they have on the political situation and the community. For the civilians who are part of this community a period of great uncertainty and fear of it's consequences begins. This fear is fed by the ignorance of what the future developments might be when abandoning the habitual way of life. Eventually this uncertain situation will transform into a new, stable situation, which gives certainty, but for a limited time. The German philosopher Hegel described this process as a dialectic system, which Fukuyama concisely summarised:

> History proceeds through a continual process of conflict, wherein systems of thought as well as political systems collide and fall apart from their own internal contradictions. They are then replaced by less contradictory and therefore higher ones, which give rise to new and different contradictions.[5]

The Concatenator is based on and developed by taking an analytical approach towards the world in which we live, in order to describe and explain the development of human behaviour. It is important to note here that we are concerned with describing the processes that are taking place. The description of these processes is essential. It has the advantage of being as objective as possible, thus avoiding a certain subjective colouring of events or concepts. In the last chapter of this part cross connections will be made of all the preceding chapters. Parallels will be struck with the first, second and third phases of the four subjects discussed, which will be projected on a more pragmatic and everyday point of view.

1 Society

1.1 Natural system

We can denote the first phase in social development as the natural phase or that of a natural system.

The history of humanity begins around 200.000 years ago. At that time Homo Sapiens, the 'wise man', arrives on the scene. An ape-man with characteristics that are much related to modern man. This species has larger brains than his predecessor, and he makes tools and builds a shelter.[6] In the earliest human civilisations, besides making tools, we also find the development of language, music, art and religion.[7] The remains that have been found on burial grounds indicate a certain degree of awareness regarding death, and perhaps the idea of an afterlife.[8]

It is a phase in the early history of humanity, in which man stands close to nature, leading a nomadic life, by hunting in small groups and by gathering food. As in nature, the earliest group culture is based on the right of the fittest. If one has a disagreement with another group member, one uses violence to regain a sense of order. In this way the argument is solved with physical strength, and as such the winner gains justice on his side. If the same member of the group wins each fight, in time this member will become the leader of the group. The other group members will then think twice to confront the leader, because they already understand the consequences from previous arguments.

In this first phase of social development it is especially our natural characteristics that count. If we are the fittest member of a group, or if we can run the fastest, we occupy a higher rank in the group. If we can escape danger more often, if we can gather more food, we gain more status in the group and more control over the group, and we will probably occupy a greater territory to watch over and profit from. Here too, The One Self is very present but at this point more on a group level: the one who has the most control, has the most power. The rest of the group is forced into submissive behaviour; they are clearly the following party. This not only has a negative effect on the followers, as they are also excused from taking the responsibility for the whole group. The moment when decisive action is needed, the followers look to the leader, who must then try to solve the problem or threat. By consequence, when he succeeds, the leader will have reaffirmed his position. Even if the group becomes bigger, the natural system remains the primal way in which to resolve disagreement within the group or with other groups, which will become more important as the groups increase in size.

So, the first types of group behaviour are established in early human existence. All members of the group compare themselves and their own achievements to the values and principles of the group. The ranking position of the group members also defines their status towards the others within the group. The higher the ranking of a group member, the more status this member has opposite other group members. This 'respect' is earned in this phase, for example, by violence, by taking heroic actions, or by establishing oneself as a leader and taking decisions for the whole group. As a consequence of this behaviour, inequality arises between the different members of the group. Bands of leaders and followers are formed to which for the greater part, there will only come an end at the end of phase 2 of the social development, as we shall see later on.

It is not surprising that group behaviour should even come about. Man is a social being: we need feedback from our fellow man about our thoughts and actions. We like to reflect our behaviour on that of others. Gather an arbitrary number of people together, and sooner or later group behaviour will be formed. We can also recognise this from our own surroundings: we feel more attracted to one person than the other, we share common interests, we feel more at ease with this person than with someone else etc. When group behaviour is formed, then rapidly some form of hierarchy will also be established. And, as soon as hierarchy is formed, people will act upon it. Hierarchy entails that one group member finds himself better, in certain areas of expertise, than other members of the group. This may work, if there is consensus on the role distribution. But it becomes less and less tolerable when some members of the group gain too much power. Various studies have shown that physical and mental violence subsequently play a role. Known examples of this are the blue and brown eyes experiment[9] and the Stanford prison experiment.[10]

It should be clear that this natural phase, where the survival of the individual is constantly threatened by members of the same species, isn't the optimal situation for man. The next step in the process of social development takes us to phase 2.

1.2 Social society

The second phase in social development is that of a social society. As we begin to manage and rule over more territory, and gradually become less dependent on the fickleness of nature, we slowly make the transformation from life in a nomadic group or clan to the first forms of sedentary civilisation. At the end of the last ice age, about 12.000 years ago, the first settlements arose and farming was developed.[11] We no longer supported ourselves by leading a nomadic life hunting and gathering food, but settled ourselves at fixed locations. Five to six thousand years ago cities arose in different places of the world, which developed independent from one another, for instance in present-day Iraq, Egypt, India, China and Mexico.[12] These settlement locations needed to be chosen as favourably as possible. As nomads we could move on when the natural resources were worn out. However this new situation had much greater consequences, because it meant that we had to leave our homes. As a result, all necessary provisions had to be available as close to the settlement as possible. For the farming of arable lands this meant at best a location close to the river in order to use the fertile soil. Examples of these are the Nile in Egypt, the Indus in India, the Euphrates and the Tigris in Iraq, and in China the Yellow River.[13] The rise of the irrigation culture is a direct consequence of this.

The cities were reinforced against invaders, which made it safer to live within the city walls than in the unprotected areas around the arable fields.[14] About this time everywhere in the world similar developments took place, again independent from one another, such as the processing of bronze, the invention of writing, the building of temples for worshipping the gods, and the crafts in general. Following this line of developments through time, states and countries arose, with a common language, history and customs as binding factors, and national culture was formed. Here it should be noted, that the idea of 'cultural nationalism' showed up for the first time in 1765. This describes an area, which, apart from its natural boundaries as mountains and rivers, is now also bound by a language or shared customs.[15]

Regarding the distribution of power, the social society initially still had one evident leader. Following phase 1 of the social development there was a supreme leader, such as a king, emperor, pharaoh, and other local variants, who surrounded himself with a court comprised of the clergy and other dignitaries. There was a middle class consisting of warriors or knights, and finally there was a class to which the farmers and other workers belonged.[16] The distribution of wealth was ordered in the same way, from high (much prosperity) to low (little prosperity). The ones at the bottom of the ladder worked to support the ruler, as for example a farmer leased a farming plot from the king, to whom he was then obliged to yield a share of the harvest. As a result of the rise in population, the supreme ruler needed the support from an increasing number of subjects to be able to justify his decisions. However it still took a few thousand years before the old hierarchy of the natural system from phase 1 was completely broken up, and power and wealth were dispersed more evenly among the people.

At the beginning of the 11th century AD, a number of critical changes took place in western Europe:

1. The economy, which until then was mainly focussed on agriculture, began to expand to other sectors of livelihood. Due to enhancements in the production process we started to change our view on nature: 'now man and nature are two things, and man is the master.'[17]
2. The taboo on money subsided, it was unbound from its sinful worldly connotations. This change in attitude strongly contributed to the rise of trades, because they were increasingly valued.[18]
3. Alongside the feudal construct of society, a communal structure developed, especially in the cities. The vertical hierarchy began to be replaced by a horizontal one, the so-called brotherhood or 'fraternitas', where the members swore allegiance to each other.[19] Much later this became one of the three pillars of the French Revolution (the other two being equality and liberty).
4. The points above brought about a feeling of status for the individual. When the professions specialised, specific knowledge was gained that could be exploited. The personal possessions and the honour the individual gained, led to a certain social position and gave the individual certain privileges. These developments form the prelude to a capitalist and more individual society.[20]

When more and more people join a communal structure, for which cities are obvious examples, mutual agreements are made. Ethics are formed with increasingly strict rules which the group observes in decision making. By then it becomes clear to the group that the 'natural' right of the fittest from phase 1, the randomness of violence that threaten all, can no longer be upheld. Rousseau describes this development as follows:

> With this view, after laying before his neighbours all the horrors of a situation, which armed them all one against another, which rendered their possessions as burdensome as their wants were intolerable, and in which no one could expect any safety either in poverty or riches, he easily invented specious arguments to bring them over to his purpose. "Let us unite," said he, "to secure the weak from oppression, restrain the ambitious, and secure to every man the possession of what belongs to him: Let us form rules of justice and peace, to which all may be obliged to conform, which shall not except persons, but may in some sort make amends for the caprice of fortune, by submitting alike the powerful and the weak to the observance of mutual duties. In a word, instead of turning our forces against ourselves, let us collect them into a sovereign power, which may govern us by wise laws, may protect and defend all the members of the association, repel common enemies, and maintain a perpetual concord and harmony among us."[21]

This transformation of power, from the natural character to the organised societal character, is a comprehensive and important step in the development of mankind. We will discuss the political consequences of this step in the next chapter. For the mutual relationships between people of the 'new' society this power transition had a more commonplace effect. The feudal society until then was based on a certain role fulfilment, of master and slave, of the oppressor and the oppressed, of power and control by one and obedience by many. In the advent of the 'democratisation' of society these mutual relationships changed.

> These democratic revolutions abolished the distinction between master and slave by making the former slaves their own masters and by establishing the principles of popular sovereignty and the rule of law. The inherently unequal recognition of masters and slaves is replaced by universal and reciprocal recognition, where every citizen recognizes the dignity and humanity of every other citizen, and where that dignity is recognized in turn by the state through the granting of *rights*.[22]

During the industrial revolution at the end of the 18th century, many farmers were initially transformed into factory workers. However, later it became clear that this new socio-economic situation, although requiring other demands, also provided new incentives for the individual. Adam Smith formulated this changed position of the individual in his publication *An Inquiry into the Nature and Causes of the Wealth of Nations* from 1776 like this: 'every man thus lives by exchanging, or becomes in some measure a merchant, and the society itself grows to be what is properly a commercial society.'[23]

Towards the end of this second phase of the social development the traditional grouping of society disappears. Then, we no longer are members of a certain religious community, a political party or another socially bound group, just because our parents were. The social control which resulted from these traditional divisions is by now loosing its grip on different sections of the population. The differences between individuals regarding race, income, power, origin, etc. -which could still lead to differentiation within the natural system of phase 1- are levelled out by the social legislation of democracy. Every individual in this democracy has the same amount of power and influence by way of rights and obligations. That is, according to the law. In practice, however, in (political) statements or in telling jokes, we can still see the recurring differentiation between groups of the population, for instance based on ones skin colour, ones faith or sexual orientation. These actually are references to the origin of a person or group, a characteristic of phase 1. When law and legislature become ever more important in the later phase of the social development, the most important functions which people can fulfil shift as well. The arguments aren't settled on the battlefields as in the natural system, but rather in court, with counsellors, judges and solicitors playing the leading roles. When we want to gain justice in a dispute we won't physically tackle someone anymore as in phase 1, but in this second phase of the social development we take 'legal measures'.

There is the idea that the industrialised societies have now come to the end of the social development. There's nothing left to enhance society or to better distribute the available resources. Another swimming pole in this municipality? More motorways? Even securer pavement for the playground recreation facilities so that the children may never ever get hurt?[24] These are mostly marginal, rather specific enhancements that don't define the 'success' of a society, they no longer are the people's fighting motives. The end of phase 2 is characterised by something which can be called equalisation through optimisation. The optimisation of social society can be witnessed in many areas in which redistribution and levelling occur. This egalitarianism decreases the differences between the people as to their rights and commitments, possibilities for development, differences in income, influence on politics, their private lives, and social life in general.

An example of the development of equalisation through optimisation can be found in the right to vote. Early on in most western democracies women didn't have the right to vote, a situation no longer sustainable in the later stage of phase 2. For, why should the rights of women differ from those of men? Why should a woman not be allowed to vote? What kind of privileges do men have that can be denied to women? The consequence is that the general rights and obligations are anchored in rules and legislature, so that any differences between the sexes, regarding the right to vote, are levelled out. Everyone is now seen and treated the same by law.

The right to vote is but one example, and it naturally also applies to the right to education, the freedom of religion and social resources for the unemployed and the ill. These are instances of the rights that have become so important to the community at the end of phase 2 that they have been included in the constitutional laws. These have become guaranties to ensure that individuals, who would otherwise be separated by differences in phase 1, are now socially fully accepted.

But does this actually mean that we are all equal, that there are absolutely no more differences to be made between individuals? If we take it from the western liberal capitalist society, then in this phase the differences in the economic situation of people will remain, which prevents the egalitarianism being fully rolled out over the whole society. Individually, we all have talents which we can use to gain certain positions in life, to be noticed, to influence our direct surroundings or a larger audience through the media. According to the law we might all be equal, but in the individual interpretation of life we all differ from one another; in this we are free.

The process of the equalisation through optimisation of the society doesn't stop at our human rights. In our social development we also want to transfer our immediate surroundings from the natural phase 1 to the social phase 2. We search for the next injustice to be equalised by optimisation. For instance, we start defending the rights of animals. Why should an animal needlessly suffer when it is slaughtered? Should we even slaughter animals? Don't animals have feelings too? When this realisation is generally accepted by a society, and legislation is adapted for it, then consequent sanctions or fines can be laid on people who wilfully harm animals.

In such a way the society evolves further into a more optimised living environment. We have access to a host of social services in the community, we have freedom of movement, materialistically we can buy what is in supply, and we can have an opinion on everything, because we can get our information from everywhere. What does there remain for a society to evolve even further?

1.3 Communication

The social development can go yet one step further. At the end of phase 2 the differences between the citizens in various areas have become minimal as a result of the established optimisation. We all have collective provisions at our disposal, and the national wealth is governmentally distributed as fair as possible, on the basis of democratically determined laws. Of course, there are still differences between individuals, but in the beginning of phase 3 these differences have been brought back to a minimum. One person, for example lives in a bit smaller or larger house than another person, but all have sufficient housing.

The following phase in the process of societal development is the self-realisation of the individual, independent of the social status which the individual has achieved in phase 2 of the social development. This third phase is called the communicative phase.

An important condition for this third phase is that the citizens can feel completely free and safe, that they can express themselves and, as it were, 'fit into' the society. The differences between the personal and the social character start to fade. Society begins to form the personal character and gives people the idea of feeling at home within society. They absorb the societal obligations into their personality.

> If an individual's character more or less closely conforms with the
> social character, the dominant drives in his personality lead him to
> do what is necessary and desirable under the specific social conditions
> of his culture.[25]

If an individual doesn't have this experience, he may have a problem with motivating himself to continue to function in this society, or lose the acknowledgement of his surroundings. This is a mutual process: society too must conform to the majority of the people.

If the character of the majority of people in a given society -that is, the social character- is thus adapted to the objective tasks the individual has to perform in this society, the energies of people are moulded in ways that make them into productive forces that are indispensable for the functioning of that society.[26]

When these conditions are met, and the individual has all the possibilities at his disposal to develop himself, then the next step is to be acknowledged by his fellow men. The individual must attract attention to himself in the company of others, the attention of other people must be drawn to the individual. Then communication must come from himself in order for others to respond to it. In this phase the technological developments have a great influence on communication. Aided by the availability and speed of data transport through the Internet, we now have a global communication channel with which we all can show our own video, vent our opinions or express anything else, at a very fast pace. Besides the Internet, there are also mobiles, ID-Cards, GPS-devices and all sorts of innovations that provide technological conditions for the communicative role we play in tomorrow's world. We make our way into an increasingly digital world. In this online or virtual space a new social structure is formed. In this new form of communication the individual is stripped of physical characteristics (whether male or female, young or old, beautiful or ugly), the geographical setting (whether at home, in the office, on the way, travelling from north to south or the other way round), the social setting (whether wealthy or poor, high or low educated), or any other 'differential' characteristic (whether black or white, homosexual or heterosexual, religious or atheistic etc.). So, in this new virtual culture it is possible to take on any identity we like, as long as we can communicate about what's on our mind, regardless of it being a one-on-one conversation with another person or via an opinion in a blog post under a pseudonym, visible to the rest of the world. Presence and immediacy rule in this communicative phase.

The search for recognition attains global proportions. The digital stage is omnipresent and potentially the whole world is watching. The data transfer in this online world effortlessly overcomes the traditional country boarders. A clear side-effect of this digital globalisation is that the cultural differences between countries appear to be less important. The social digital conventions, applied by all users of the technological inventions, take care of further exchange and the adaptation of cultural differences.

> The unfolding of modern natural science has had a uniform effect on all societies that have experienced it [...]. Modern natural science establishes a uniform horizon of economic production possibilities. Technology makes possible the limitless accumulation of wealth, and thus the satisfaction of an ever-expanding set of human desires. This process guarantees an increasing homogenization of all human societies, regardless of their historical origins or cultural inheritances. All countries undergoing economic modernization must increasingly resemble one another: they must unify nationally on the basis of a centralized state, urbanize, replace traditional forms of social organization like tribe, sect, and family with economically rational ones based on function and efficiency, and provide for the universal education of their citizens. Such societies have become increasingly linked with one another through global markets and the spread of a universal consumer culture.[27]

The last step in this phase will focus more on content than form, on the immediacy of information or the technological possibilities. All the conditions of the former phases have been met, and now the focus will lie on the self-realisation of each individual. All possibilities of the early stage of this phase remain, but their attraction now has less impact than it once had. The individuals within a society in the last stage of this phase strive for the inner perfection of all that makes us human, based on self-knowledge, insight and self-control. It is a yearning for optimised self-realisation, fitted with all the benefits of the former phases, and convinced of a virtuous life in a well-balanced society.

However, it doesn't mean that this phase always takes place at the end of the total societal process. Several moments in history can be pointed out that already show signs of this phase. At the beginning of the 19th century we find the Bohemians. The followers of this free-thinking movement averted themselves from the mediocrity of the working class, the population in phase 2 of the social development. These free-thinkers strived for original human behaviour, where artistry and truthfulness were more important than the accumulation of wealth and the achievement of status.[28] We find a similar response at the end of the 18th century with Romanticism. In response to the Industrial Revolution and the political and aristocratic values of that age, the Romanticists, also found refuge in the arts and especially in painting, music and literature. Besides this, Romanticism was also a rejection of the concurrent scientific view of the world, which gained attention simultaneously. The hard and cold facts, the search for the objective truth that science presents, are of no importance to the Romanticists. The subjectiveness in human beings is far more important to them, as everything can be true to the individual, and truth is not universal.[29]

2 Politics

2.1 The Dictator

The moment a large group of people choose a fixed location to work the land and so part with a nomadic existence, the process of power distribution, out of which a certain hierarchy develops, gains a new impulse. The first forms of hierarchy are based on the right of the fittest. The leader of the group, the chief or village elder is in charge and takes the decisions for the whole group. Later, when the territory and the group increase, and when certain group identity is formed, which can be described as a tribe, a people or a culture, the status and power of the tribe leader increase as well. This leader is promoted, or he promotes himself, to for example a king, pharaoh or emperor. While these groups still function on the basis of the strength of the fittest, we had now better call him a dictator, an authoritarian person who solely determines what decisions to take, that apply to the whole group. With the increase of the population more products are needed, and people begin to specialise in their role, of course all in the service of the dictator. Different trades and functions develop creating further levels in the existing hierarchy. In making contact with the gods there's the high priest or the medicine man. In ruling the army there's a commander. And there are -in this phase of the social development as well- many farmers and labourers at the bottom of the hierarchy. The dictator thus rules over an ever growing number of people in an ever increasing hierarchical kingdom. But he cannot go too far in exploiting his own people, as that would provoke a coup. A way to avert this danger is to wage a war against a rival tribe. Apart from preventing a foreign invasion, a victory would give the whole population a moral boost and would reaffirm the leadership of the dictator. However, parallel to phase 1 of the social development, the dictator still finds himself within the natural system, in which he must be aware of internal threats, such as scores settled between individuals within the group to work oneself up a rung on the hierarchical ladder.

The dictator can stay on his throne as long as he remains powerful enough, as long as his oppression and reputation have effect. Eventually, however, this will end, by a foreign attack from a stronger people for instance, or when the dissatisfaction within one or more groups in the hierarchy becomes too great. The dictator then cannot maintain his leading position, others will stake claim to their share of power in the next phase of social development.

2.2 Democracy

At a certain moment the dictator cannot maintain his empire which is based on his own strength and the loyalty of his court. At the beginning of this second political phase he starts to lose his power over the people. Too weak a leader, an obvious corrupt system, strife among the leading men, or a population which begins to understand the increasing inequity of its existence. These are some of the factors that can push the dictator off his throne and induce the people to claim part of the power. Through the fall of the dictator, the court, as well as the priests and the commanders lose their influence. Previously the power, knowledge and access to information were gathered in the top section of the hierarchy, but now the population also slowly gains access to them. A political transition takes place, from the exclusive rights of the dictator to the common rights for all. But in doing so the individual gives up his natural freedom in favour of social security.

> The passage from the state of nature to the civil state produces a very remarkable change in man, by substituting justice for instinct in his conduct, and giving his actions the morality they had formerly lacked. Then only, when the voice of duty takes the place of physical impulses and right of appetite, does man, who so far had considered only himself, find that he is forced to act on different principles, and to consult his reason before listening to his inclinations. [...] What man loses by the social contract is his natural liberty and an unlimited right to everything he tries to get and succeeds in getting; what he gains is civil liberty and the proprietorship of all he possesses. If we are to avoid mistake in weighing one against the other, we must clearly distinguish natural liberty, which is bounded only by the strength of the individual, from civil liberty, which is limited by the general

> will; and possession, which is merely the effect of force or the right
> of the first occupier, from property, which can be founded only on a
> positive title.[30]

With the disappearance of the dictator from phase 1 the central power and authority disappear as well. As soon as the process leading to phase 2 is set in motion, going back to phase 1 seems quite unlikely, as the cards have been played out for the most part. However, history has shown that a relapse into phase 1 can occur several times, especially in the very beginning of phase 2. But, looking at the number of monarchies worldwide, we see a great decrease in the last 150 years, and the ones in existence today mostly fulfil a ceremonial function.

Public access to information is a very important aspect in the transformation into a democratic society. The invention of book printing in western Europe for instance accounts for a wider and faster spread of information. More people learn to read and write, and in doing so gain knowledge. They are no longer dependent on the authorities who put forward a certain, usually coloured, message. The process of information dissemination has had a great influence on the development of science, and later on the industrialisation. With a population which is more often and better informed, and which is increasingly able to speak up and claim the right to equal treatment, the political system also goes through a big transformation: unions arise, as well as advisory bodies, committees, opportunities for public comment, etc. A different political system is necessary, in which the whole population can influence general decision making. A written law proves to suit this new power distribution best. When the population sets in writing by which rules they want to be bound, the citizens can address one another when they break the law. One of the starting points in arranging such a fundamental law, a constitution, is the principle: don't do unto others what you don't want others to do unto you.

> The only purpose for which power can be rightfully exercised over any
> member of a civilised community against his will, is to prevent harm
> to others. His own good, either physical or moral, is not a sufficient
> warrant. He cannot rightfully be compelled to do or forbear because it
> will be better for him to do so, because it will make him happier, be-
> cause, in the opinion of others, to do so would be wise, or even right.[31]

The reciprocity of desired behaviour is like holding up a mirror to the community and a safeguard against murder and theft -actions that belong to the dictatorship in phase 1. This is an instrument to help individuals to think first about the consequences of their actions and to begin to control themselves. Common sense, laid down in laws, wins it in this phase of natural human impulses. In the constitution a set of basic conditions are formulated, for example that all individuals are equal, regardless of the sex, skin colour etc. Although it isn't automatically reflected in reality, it is nonetheless settled within legislature, and in the event of a dispute every individual can appeal to equal treatment.

Which political system connects best to this development depends on which country you look at. Democracy, oligarchy, theocracy, liberalism, socialism, communism, monarchy and authoritarian regimes are a number of representatives of political systems. These are systems in which the power to take the peoples' decisions has been structured.

In most western countries this political transition is marked by the rise of the modern democracy. This new governmental state arose during the rule of king Louis XIV in France at the end of the 17th century.[32] The rise of a democracy clearly marks the transition from phase 1 to phase 2 in the political development. An important aspect of democracy is that the dictatorial power over a nation is curbed and dispersed more evenly over the population, which means one man for one vote in a parliamentary democracy. Via free elections the citizens can state their political preference, and thus transfer the power to the chosen representatives of the political debate. The population is no longer managed hard handily, such as in phase 1. In phase 2 of the political development common laws reign instead. There are duties the citizens must observe, but they also have rights they can appeal to. Since the end of the 18th century, with two important instigations in the American and French Revolution, the number of democracies combined with a liberal economy has risen immensely worldwide.[33]

In phase 2 of the social development we have seen that at the beginning of the 12th century the European economy changes, that earning money is no longer taboo, that fraternities are formed and individual strive for status emerges. All these elements combine and exert themselves in the 14th and 15th century as the Renaissance, with the Italian city of Florence at its centre, and where a combination of commerce and art make way to a new era. For the first time all the ingredients of the future political and economical situation in Europe and other parts of the world come together: capitalism, free commerce, liberalism and a democratic political system.

The free market philosophy of capitalism fits within the liberal character of the democratic system. It is an economic system that works on the basis of investments into certain products, with an expected profit margin for the producer, most often in the form of a private enterprise with employees on wages. The product produced, is traded for a market price, mostly based on the scarcity of products. This scarcity determines offer and demand, thus the price of a product on the free market. Capitalism is an economic system in which the individual works for an accumulation of possessions. For the employer this has a favourable effect on productivity. Because, the more, the faster or the better an employee works, the more products the employer can develop, generating a new stream of income. This in turn is good for the general economy. This requires of course that the consumers and producers keep cooperating, so that the economic cycle of expenses and investments remains viable. There is an obvious downside to this system. For it is very focussed on the personal gain of mainly material possessions, and the number of possessions is supposed to keep equal pace with the measure of personal happiness. We will return later to this so-called hedonic treadmill.

From the Industrial Revolution onwards it becomes possible to transform resources on a large scale into what we call desired products. There is now a sense of control or victory of man over nature. The cities begin to play an ever prominent role in this. The rural community, especially the low volume their handicraft produces, can no longer compete with the large scale productions by steam engines in the factories. A massive migration of rural workers to the cities takes place. At first they work in the factories under miserable conditions, later on unions are established to protect the interests of these workers. This last century capitalism has had an enormous influence on the whole of society, as Fromm sums up in short:

> The disappearance of feudal traits, the revolutionary increase in indus-
> trial production, the increasing concentration of capital and bigness
> of business and government, the increasing number of people who
> manipulate figures and people, the separation of ownership from man-
> agement, the rise of the working class economically and politically,
> the new methods of work in factory and office.[34]

The concepts of democracy, liberalism and capitalism are closely knit with each other. If the democratic principles aren't met, it will become quite difficult to make that step towards liberalism. And without involvement in the decision making and the acknowledgement of equal rights, we can hardly speak of a free market such as in a liberal society. When free trade is absent on the economic market, we can't actually speak of the existence of conditions necessary for a capitalist society. In a liberal society the people are free to make their own choices, resulting in a great variety of (economic) activities. In a deregulated capitalist market there will also be an increase in the difference between the lowest and the highest incomes.[35]

On the other hand, the process of equalisation through optimisation will lead to a certain social revolution. Slowly all the elements, that lead to too much inequality between citizens, will become redundant or will be replaced by a practically levelled social society. It is apparent to want to regulate this evolution and subsequently establish bodies to control the regulation. The effect of this is a multitude of foundations, hallmarks, consumer organisations, union organisations, committees, independent research bureaus, participation rounds, etc. This enormous participation in the democratic system stimulates the development of an optimal social situation, but on the down side this leads to a mass of bureaucratic institutions. It does however prevent extreme political parties from gaining ground: before they've taken all the bureaucratic hurdles, the storm has usually already set.

The combination of liberalism and capitalism leads to an ever growing entrepreneurial market. A free trafficking of goods, people and capital, along with the possibility of setting up private enterprises in a global market, leads to the globalisation of commerce. Further into the development of phase 2 another political model will appear, the technocracy.

2.3 Technocracy

The end of phase 2 in the political development is characterised by a decrease in the differences among people socially, politically and economically. By law in any case, we are all equal, and there are no more distinctions between individuals regarding the choice of religion, sexual orientation, political preference, etc. As an effect of the process of equalisation through optimisation at the end of phase 2 everyone is accepted as an individual, and the personal preferences are respected. For, if the society doesn't tolerate this, the differences will then be pointed out, and individuals will be discriminated, which it has been agreed upon by law to abstain from. The discrimination does not correspond with the process of equalisation through optimisation achieved at the end of phase 2. Each individual is thus treated as an equal at the beginning of phase 3, in a society in which the same social resources are available to everyone.

Now, after the democratic political system combined with the capitalist economic model, as described in the previous chapter, what would be the next phase? Among the most important instigators of phase 3 in the political development will be the results of scientific research. Begun in phase 2 as the scientific revolution, in phase 3 scientific research will progress further through new technological inventions and discoveries. A society at the end of phase 2 is already highly provisioned with technology. An average household has a variety of technical devices at its disposal, such as mobile phones, computers, kitchen appliances, televisions, right up to the electric garage door and lawn mower. We quickly get used to the luxuries these devices afford us, and it's always a small step to the next generation with just a few more technical possibilities.

The same goes for various other sectors, such as the health services, transport, and science in general, which make use of improved, more specific and/or more expensive devices to arrive at new discoveries or to work more efficiently.

The progress made within these technological resources also ensures that the individual can easily come into contact with others, who may be dispersed over the whole world. In this limitless digital world a national government has very little influence left on the behaviour of the communicating global citizen, even though upholding the law is a primal function of the controlling government. In this technocratic society a government is no longer focussed on following a certain ideology. At the beginning of phase 3 the differences between population groups have become minimised in many areas and their interests have mostly become the same. The political power in charge constitutes of a knowledge cabinet comprising ministers who are the best at their trade. Technological developments and scientific research provide the foundation and the motivation for the policies made. Considering the progress in technological developments, the marginalisation of ideology within society, and the ceaseless communication of individuals, a technocracy may well be the governmental form that best suits this phase in the political development.

It also is the most logical next step at the end of phase 2. The interplay between democracy, liberalism and capitalism is necessary to achieve the globalisation of commerce. The free trafficking of goods, people and capital, the possibility of setting up a private enterprise in a global market, the process of equalisation by optimisation (in the economical and in the ideological sense), propelled by technological developments and open to the individual recognition of every citizen, these are a few elements that make heading towards a technocratic society rather easy.

3 Religion

3.1 Awe and worship

In every culture on earth we can find some form of religion. Although perhaps it's better to place the concept of religion within a wider context and to speak of convictions of life, that since long gave man a sense of security on the important but intangible matters of life. In the early days of human existence there were many inexplicable phenomena: nature's harshness, with its destructive powers displayed by earthquakes, lightning, and floods, the daily struggle for food harnessed by an inner urge to survive, and ultimately the mysterious death. But, set against this is nature's beauty, the nourishing rain and the warmth of the sun, both necessary for crop growing fields providing a successful harvest. All in all it must have been an wondrous experience for early humans, looking up every night at the starlit sky.

When we finally shed our natural skin and our conscience started growing, we began asking questions about this strange, hostile, inexplicable world. How do we explain this impressive environment? Why do we exist? What will happen with us after we die? In the early phases of human history there were no ready answers for these questions. Religion, however, provided for a fitting alternative. In this first phase man stood close to nature, and when agriculture started providing for the staple diet, religion and especially certain gods, reflected its importance: a god for the rain to make the soil fertile, a god for the sun, to let everything flourish, a god for a good harvest to provide people with their daily bread.[36] Man was dependent on the fickleness of nature, and man tried to gain control over it by worshipping the gods.

Religion was our initial onset in order to explain the inexplicable in the world around us and to gain answers to the most important questions in life. Most of what we saw and experienced we found inexplicable, and together with our inner wonder about all kinds of natural events, these formed the basis of religion, resulting in awe and worship of the unknown higher powers.

The relationship between the gods and humans has always been close. God cannot be a completely different being, one that we cannot relate to. Our humanity *must* be reflected in a creating god, otherwise we can never build a recognisable bond with it, we can't identify with it. Xenophanes of Colophon already stated as much around 500 BC: 'if horses could draw, they would draw their gods like horses.'[37]

In many early cultures we find a person who, as a mediator, had contact with the gods. This mediator, embodied by the medicine man, high priest, druid, shaman, prophet, oracle, etc., could ask the gods for advice or request a favour of them. In this way he could support the dictator from phase 1 of the social development in taking important decisions. This resulted in a dictator's decision determining how to influence the people to achieve the desired behaviour. This can be seen as the beginning of setting values and principles, implemented at a group level. This inherently led to what can be seen as 'good' and 'bad' behaviour. The behaviour of an individual within a group could now be evaluated: if it wasn't in line with enforced rules the individual could be punished.

Besides this the high priest was involved in the most important events in life. Birth, marriage and death each mark a transitional phase, which needs the approval of the higher powers, and which is accompanied by certain rituals. Thus, the high priest had a unique and powerful position, by enforcing these ethical behavioural rules. Especially also, because the people had no access to the information of the high priest, and so couldn't think or act differently. By consequence, the dictator was also largely dependent on the high priest, until the moment, when the high priest made a wrong prediction once too many. The dictator could then decide to exploit the circumstance by eliminating the high priest, thereby reasserting his authority.

So, the history of religions first of all begins from within nature. Animism represents religions in which people stand close to nature, and where the gods are to be found on the highest mountain, beyond the far horizon, in the deepest lake, in everything that was awe inspiring or unapproachable. Later a more 'personal' bond with the gods is established. Archaeologists have made many finds of pictorial and sculptural renditions of bulls and women with broad hips and big breasts, both symbols of fertility.[38] Religious ideas were projected onto an object, which could subsequently be worshipped. Much later religion also exerts itself on the legislative and social aspects of society by preaching legislation, values and principles. This is most prominent in the patriarchal religions. The development of religions of course isn't as strict as outlined here. Religions most often adopts elements of other religions, and some movements, such as polytheism, remain in existence even today and are not automatically replaced by monotheistic patriarchal religions.

The period in which most of the global religions are established is called the Axial Age, which roughly dates from 800 to 200 BC.[39] In this period arise for instance Christianity in the Middle East, Buddhism and Jainism in India, Confucianism and Taoism in China and Shintoism in Japan. A few religions were already established earlier, the most conspicuous ones of those were Zoroastrianism and Judaism in the Middle East and Hinduism in India. Also in this Axial Period, we see the rise of reason in ancient Greece, with such philosophers as Socrates, Plato and Archimedes.

Religions lie at the base of every culture and, local variations aside, they usually all possess a common set of elements:

> A belief in the Great Goddess, in the Bull, in the main sky gods (the sun and the moon), in sacred stones, in the efficacy of sacrifice, in an afterlife, and in a soul of some sort which survives death and inhabits a blessed spot.[40]

Religious scientists distinguish similar main characteristics for every religion: doctrine, mythology, religious experience, institutionalisation, ethical or practical instructions, rituals, sacred objects and places.[41]

Essentially, religion prescribes a set of rules, by which it is attempted to explain the world as it should be, and these rules are used to regulate the way we should live. By following these values and principles, we can live on after death, thereby surpassing the natural limits of our own temporary, earthly body to a status of transcendence, of transfiguration into a celestial domain. The way in which people are obliged to live corresponds with the world view a religion presents. In most religions this world consists of a metaphysical, eternal world above the physical and temporary world, which is our everyday experience. Mostly these religions contain one or more gods, which represent the perfection that people strive for. In this way an image is formed of one or more gods, representing the opposite of what people are and are capable of: humans are temporary, the gods are eternal; humans possess limited knowledge, the gods know everything; humans are captives of their own bodies, the gods are as free as ghosts; humans die here on earth, the gods live on in a celestial realm. As such religion provides answers to the important, inexplicable phenomena in this life, for instance the death of a fellow man, where it provides people consolation and a glimpse of life after this earthly one.

3.2 Science

As we've seen in chapter 1 at phase 2 of the social development, at a certain moment the dictator looses his influence, and so does the religious medium. The social and political system from phase 1 is overthrown, and room is created to build up a new system in its stead. With this, the people re-evaluate their situation and ask themselves anew how the world should be explained in their daily activities and circumstances. In this second phase of the religious development information is not just accessible to the highest ranks in the social hierarchy, but rather to the entire population. More and more people can read and write. Of course this is a gradual process, but finally this results in more independent knowledgeable individuals with their own opinions. The contents of religious writings or deliveries of oral traditions are no longer indiscriminately held true.

Instead of establishing a new religion or adapting existing religions following new developments in this second phase, science steps in with a description of common reality. This view on reality is also rooted in certain assumptions, but those are now based on empirical, experimental research. Alternatively put: the natural sciences are based on conducting experiments, which must be able to be tested to the same results anywhere in the world. A natural scientific hypothesis must conclusively result in verifiable proof. When a new hypothesis is refuted, then the existing laws remain. But if this new hypothesis is confirmed, then the old laws are abandoned and replaced by new ones. If this new law has far-reaching consequences for science as a whole, then we may speak of a scientific revolution.

At the beginning of the 13th century a first step towards a systematic description of reality, as it suits our present idea of this approach, already took place.[42] This new study of the world was based on a number of developments which occurred in western society between 1000 and 1100 AD, and which also had an impact on the way religion was experienced within society.

Firstly, the individual breaks with the group. Now, more than before, personal considerations or feelings are conveyed, for instance in poetry, sculptures become more lifelike -less abstract-, and for the first time the artist expresses his sense of pride for his own work. Bound to his pride is a yearning for acknowledgement, the artist wants to make himself known to the world, considering that making a nameless sculpture for God's glory no longer suffices.[43] The personal honour and self-enrichment set about a different view on the earthly here and now. Suddenly, there are things in this life worth striving for, in any case in business or in artistry. Later, and under the influence of Protestantism, this development leads to the secularisation of belief all around Europe. To practice faith the conveyance by the church or priest is no longer needed. Instead, the texts from the Bible formed a new individual compass. Now, the religious conviction is disconnected from the societal and political system. The earthly leader no longer is the most important embodiment of the heavenly domains. This development paves the way to a liberal society.[44]

Secondly, there is the rise of capitalism. The cities and states keep on growing. Consequently different trades form outside the clerical realm, such as teaching, counselling, clerking for the court or parliaments. New agricultural techniques develop by which produce increase with 50%. Around 1200 AD clocks appear on the bell towers, which allow work to be quantified. From this moment on the yields of harvest can be accurately related to the number of working hours. Watermills provide for the textile industry. This combination of factors results in an increase in trade on the markets, the monetary system gains a prominent role and leads to the idea of capital.[45] Through an increase in material wealth individuals become less inclined to listen to the message religion proclaims about a metaphysical salvation, which occurs somewhere else and at a later time.

The next great development, influencing the role of religion in society, occurs halfway through the 16th century, when the Polish astronomer Nicolaus Copernicus publishes his vision on the universe. In doing so, he replaces the existing geocentric model of Ptolemy -in which the earth occupies the centre of the universe- with a new heliocentric model, where the sun is at the centre and the earth is one of the planets revolving around it. Apart from being a new model, it is especially the psychological blow to humanity that continues to resonate. Man no longer stands at the centre of the cosmos, we are but beings on one of the many planets which spin around the sun. And, as if that's not enough, the first scientific revolution, lasting until the middle of the 18th century, provides even more new insights, such as: the discovery of gravity, the structure of light, the vacuum, gasses, the human body, and microscopic life formed by bacteria. The second scientific revolution, starting in 1900, adds to it the discovery of the quantum world, genes and the subconscious.[46]

Resulting from this new, scientific, explanation of the world around us, the religious systems from phase 1 receive a different interpretation. Individuals living in a society within phase 2, are no longer frightened by lightning as though it were divine intervention, a 'godly roar'. Many of these everyday phenomena are studied and explained by science, reducing the influence religion has on society.

The foundation laid down by religions in phase 1 of the religious development can be seen as a basis for a society in phase 2. The ethical rules from phase 1, on how to live with each other, are set in a general constitution in phase 2, and are thus supported by the whole community. However, this doesn't mean that ethical behaviour or morality only rely on religion as a source or only belong to humankind. It is known that animals too are capable of altruistic behaviour.[47]

3.3 What is left?

The solidarity the group felt by practising religion in phase 1 of the religious development, can no longer be sustained in phase 2. The central role religion fulfilled in society decreases due to the scientific revolution and the rise of a welfare society. At the end of phase 2 of the religious development life convictions gain an increasingly individual approach. Individuals develop their own opinions of certain values and principles, develop their own vision towards life, but of course within the boundaries of the law, that society purposefully set in phase 2 of the social development. In phase 3 of the religious development the mental self-realisation is pushed even further, where it becomes less obvious to be guided by rules of a coordinating organisation, such as the church. Even though, here too, the experiences relative to the personal interpretation of a life conviction are increased by discussion in a group. The affirmation of individual choice and the recognition of an individual by others remain important issues.

In this phase no new religions are formed to address large groups with a general message, those actually only arise in phase 1, in the Axial Age as we've seen before. However, new religious movements do arise, led for instance by a personal mentor or a guru, who, by means of modern communication methods, spreads his message relatively quickly and easily all over the world. Although, this could also have a counter effect. It is possible that these new life convictions will be scrutinised by the media, immediately revealing misinformation, deceit or other negative developments.

In this third phase, religion will still remain a projection of all that we are not or can not be, a longing for perfection. That which isn't tangible to us, such as trust, hope, the future or a possible life after death, ensures that we remain on a quest for answers. By research and the resulting explanations, the sciences may restrain the possibilities of religion, however the human longing for meaningfulness or a destination will never be explained in this way, nor will it disappear. Giving meaning to the most important questions of life, the aim of a meaningful life, hope and reassurance, these will always belong to the domain of a life conviction. Future science can make little change to that as well. Thus, the divine will always remain intangible, a source or object of questioning.

4 The Individual

4.1 Craft

At the beginning of phase 1 of the individual development, every person has a role, task or function to fulfil within a distinct group. The individual lives close to nature and fights to survive, to provide for a daily meal. The next step in this development is the formation of tribes, where the individual participates in a larger group. This is partly at the cost of individuality, as the individual's voice is less heard. On the upside, however, the group can provide for better protection of the individual. Occurring conflicts no longer take place at an individual level within the group, but at a group level, the battles are now fought between tribes. The individual is now mostly identified with his own tribe. As we've seen before, the right of the fittest is paramount in this first phase, and the members of the tribe obey the decisions of the tribal chief. In early civilisations human blood flows heavily if only to reaffirm the tribal head's right to the throne or to appease the gods by making sacrifices. In this phase certain knowledge resides mainly with the tribal leader, his dignitaries, the village elder(s), and the medium who comes into contact with the spiritual world. The individual is generally excluded from any form of knowledge transfer or communication on the more significant subjects, which remains a privilege of the court. In this phase the individual knowledge development, which is mostly based on one's own experiences, is often orally transmitted to the next generations.

In this first phase the individual development is largely dependent on his own hands. Man fights animals with his bare hands, and later he uses self-made tools to aide in killing the animals during hunting. A pair of hands afford man to gather and prepare food, build shelter and make fire. Our hands aide us in ruling over this world. The increase in brain power effectuated in the application of tools, and the ability to communicate with members of the same species of course go hand-in-hand. What we can think up in our minds, we make with our hands. When man progresses further, and leaves the nomadic life behind, he first settles at strategic locations where the soil is fertile and nature is divers enough to sustain himself. Later on, these settlements will develop into villages and cities. Everything here is done by brute muscle power, and, according to modern standards, with very little resources. The process of the individual development is still in phase 1, equal to the natural phase of the social development. With his bare hands man literally shapes the world around him. We still find testimonies to this in many inscriptions chiselled into or painted on rock faces all around the world, as attested by the ancient civilisations of e.g. the Egyptians, the Aboriginals in Australia or the Maya in Middle-America.

The further the developments proceed in this phase, the more refined the handicraft becomes, and the first professions arise, which are later called trades.[48] In various cultures we see e.g. carpenters, stone masons and smithies appear working in their workshops. They supply a growing demand for specific products. Until a few hundred years ago trades were the prime motive behind human development. Products around the world were produced in the same, laborious manner. This would change for good at the advent of the industrial revolution.

4.2 The Service Manager

In phase 2 of the individual development the dictator no longer bears the sceptre. His authoritarian grip on his subjects has disappeared, and the role of the individuals becomes more important. For, the individuals begin to develop a feeling of self-worth. In the transition between phases 1 and 2 the structure the dictator had established, the court, the clerical order and the military power, gradually disappear. The strict segregation of social classes within the various societal groups gradually dissolves as well. As an effect of which individuals begin positioning themselves on the social ladder. And, science matures and gains a more central position in human development, more knowledge, more information becomes available on an individual level. The invention of the printing press, the first news papers, the first encyclopedia, these are examples of how knowledge from documented information spread relatively quickly the world over. Reading and writing come within reach of every man, in turn leading to an increase in knowledge and progress at an individual level.

The trades, that arose through handicraft in phase 1, lose their certainty of existence in phase 2, when the costs outrun the production quantities. By the end of the 18th century, when the industrial revolution is in full swing, many people have moved to the cities to work in the large factories, leading to a decrease in agricultural labourers. In the factories, the activities of the workers, which is what they become, consist mainly of assembly line production. To continue gaining the same profit, the production must increase and the work must gain efficiency. Later the work, consisting of repetitious activities, is taken over by machines. Eventually, machines are developed to build machines, the assembly robot takes over the majority of the tasks done by human hand.

The developments in the industrialised countries also influence the professions people have in such a society. The role of management gains importance: the manager must guard the production process, and where needed, intervene in time. This is necessary, because, as with the factories, the projects keep increasing in size and complexity, and the amount of production increases as well. There's also a research and development department coming up with new products, a public relations department guarding the brand image of the company, and a marketing department positioning the new products on the market. Increasingly less people deliver work made by their own hands. In their stead, factory halls are filled with automated machinery and there's just one person left in the control room to keep watch over the production line. The unique idea for a new product, the innovation, and the accompanying patents become increasingly more important at the end of phase 2. As with the trades in phase 1, a new specialisation of knowledge and skills now takes place.

> The unremitting division of labour resulted in admirable levels of productivity. The company's success appeared to bear out the principles of efficiency laid down at the turn of the twentieth century by the Italian economist Vilfredo Pareto, who theorised that a society would grow wealthy to the extent that its members forfeited general knowledge in favour of fostering individual ability in narrowly constricted fields. In an ideal Paretan economy, jobs would be ever more finely subdivided to allow for the accumulation of complex skills, which would then be traded among workers.[...] In a perfect society, so specialised would all jobs be, that no one would any longer understand what anyone else was doing.[49]

As mentioned in part one, our knowledge and insight into the world around us become increasingly specific. We gain knowledge, which in turn produces new questions, followed by a search for new answers. This increasing specification of our world view also applies to our working process. Simple and physical work, consisting of clear continuously repetitive activities, are taken over by a machine, in this case a robot. The more mental tasks, such as model calculation, statistic data processing etc., are also taken over by a machine, and this time by a computer. Work that we do ourselves becomes more specific, we increasingly become authorities, specialists at our own work field. The diversity in knowledge and insight, and simultaneously the number of professional titles, increase further. In the specialisation of our own work field, there is a danger that our contact with the 'real' world, the daily reality, will be obscured. This is evident, when in daily socialising it becomes ever more difficult to explain to someone else what our function entails, what we're actually doing.

At the end of phase 2 we all more or less fulfil the role of a manager. Albeit at work or at home, by having to deal with quite a number of things, keeping contact with all kinds of institutions, and maintaining socially desirable behaviour which has become expected of the individual by the media and our fellow man. At the end of this second phase the individual is part of a society that operates as one large servicing company.

But, if we're all functioning as service managers, then who's serving who?

4.3 Consuming

In the digital communicative world in phase 3 of the individual development, people have most often become managers. They pass on information from point A to point B. From a professional point of view this is mostly management information: what does the customer want? How does the customer want it? How much does the customer want? For how much can he afford it? When does he want to use it, if not why, and what would he choose instead? By optimising the production process companies are compelled to compete with each other on very narrow profit margins. In this process every detail of customer information can be decisively important to maintain, let alone increase, the product sale rate.[50] This abundance of information corresponds with the third communicative phase of the social development described in chapter 1. In this phase trade results, media and image become key factors for companies and consumers alike.

A consequence is that the individual actually 'does' less and less physically. This is to say: we produce increasingly less by means of physical labour, we less often set to work at something physically compared to phase 1 of the individual development. We more often take our place at a computer or in front of a television screen. Provided with all kinds of modern conveniences, such as household appliances, we hardly need to stop to think about anything any more, we become lazy, become bored more quickly and are very hard to motivate. Via the internet all information can be found immediately. Due to the globalisation, the originally seasonal and regional products have become available everywhere, all year round. In this phase the individual actually only needs to consume.

> It is not difficult to recognize the widespread longing for the state of complete laziness and passivity. Our advertising appeals to it even more than to sex. There are, of course, many useful and labor saving gadgets. But this usefulness often serves only as a rationalization for the appeal to complete passivity and receptivity. A package of breakfast cereal is being advertised as "*new – easier to eat.*" An electric toaster is advertised with these words: "… the most distinctly different toaster in the world! Everything is done *for* you with this new toaster. You need not even bother to lower the bread. Power-action, though a unique electric motor, *gently takes the bread right out of your fingers!*" How many courses in languages, or other subjects are announced with the slogan "effortless learning, no more of the old drudgery." Everybody knows the picture of the elderly couple in the advertisement of a life-insurance company, who have retired at the age of sixty, and spend their life in the complete bliss of having nothing to do except just travel.[51]

Society provides its citizens with all kinds of public amenities, and many products have been completely thought through and perfectly finished: behind every product there's a marketing model, everything has exactly the right, artificial, taste one expects, and it comes in the best possible wrapping. The whole production and marketing process is based on efficiency, predictability, calculability, manageability, what George Ritzer describes as the McDonaldisation of the community.[52] The consumers need only follow market conform demand and find their answers in a new, attractive, product.

> The most obvious illustration of this principle is to be found in our system of buying on the installment plan. In the nineteenth century

> you bought what you needed, when you had saved the money for it;
> today you buy what you need, or do not need, on credit, and the func-
> tion of advertising is largely to coax you into buying and to whet your
> appetite for things, so that you can be coaxed. You live in a circle. You
> buy on the installment plan, and about the time you have finished
> paying, you sell and you buy again – the latest model.[53]

The optimised society, thus, is one mainly in which the economy has been completely evolved. Beside it's collective advantages, it also brings a great disadvantage for the individual, which is the alienation of that same society. In a society where technology plays such a decisive role, and where efficiency is key, the human measure -embodied in the possibility of doubt, of failure, of a deviation from the norm- and thus the identity of the individual can become pressured. Man strays ever more away from his natural decent. In our work, we are responsible for just one element of the whole process, and we often don't see the final product. And, in our private lives we live in a city without personality, where there is no place left for harbouring child-hood memories.

> The attitude towards work has the quality of instrumentality; in con-
> trast to a medieval artisan the modern manufacturer is not primarily
> interested in what he produces; he produces essentially in order to
> make a profit from his capital investment, and what he produces de-
> pends essentially on the market which promises that the investment
> of capital in a certain branch will prove to be profitable.[54]

This alienation from the natural environment has physical and mental consequences for the consuming individual. Obesity, ADHD, RSI, burn-out, depression, borderline, these are all phenomena of the new strongly indus-trialised and optimised society, where the individual performs his profession to earn a living. This is a very different situation from what we've seen in phase 1, where the clinical conditions or even causes of death are much more natural in character, such as infections and diseases like malaria.[55, 56] In phase 3 of the individual development there's also a greater role for the individual in social communication. Virtual meeting places of like-minded people, sharing personal preferences on social media websites, and passing on news that could be of national importance, these are instances of the new digital social structures that arise beside the existing 'analogue' structures. Here, the immediacy reigns, for all information is continuously available through the internet and mobile devices, and can be shared at once amid one's acquaintances.

In phase 3 of the individual development the social differences also further diminish. The class differences between an erudite, aristocratic scholar from phase 2 and a 'lesser literate' person from phase 3 have fallen away by continuous access to the online knowledge bank. One can drown in this immeasurable ocean of possibilities. In using online communication methods there's a continuous presence of a worldwide stage, with permanently sold-out seats. However, with so many actors competing on this stage, it will become increasingly difficult to find individual recognition.

At such a moment the individual, who has reached all his goals, and who is furnished with all conveniences, will turn inwards as the only remaining alternative step. What's important here too is that, within a society in phase 2, individuals come of age before completely fulfilling their consumptive needs. Only later in life do they find the time to ask themselves what use or goal life has. In phase 3, when prosperity has greatly increased, an individual will have achieved many of his 'goals' at a much younger age: he is financially independent, he has possessions the acquisition of which was self-motivated (or motivated by others). Materialistically he's successful. Thus, he also has an earlier opportunity to ask himself what his life's aim is, and what more he could want. He might then jump-start doing useful rather that necessary work. This mental self-development requires reflection on the present individual situation and an inner motive for a more conscientious, balanced way of life. With this, the individual acknowledgement and appreciation can return to every person's domain, and can even take up a central position.

By then we will have gained total freedom. However coping with this new situation won't be that obvious. Throughout all the previous phases we've freed ourselves from our natural restraints, religious dogma's, and social group behaviour, but internally there's still a world to discover, as Fromm describes:

> We are proud that in his conduct of life man has become free from external authorities, which tell him what to do and what not to do. We neglect the role of the anonymous authorities like public opinion and "common sense", which are so powerful because of our profound readiness to conform to the expectations everybody has about ourselves and our equally profound fear of being different. In other words, we are fascinated by the growth of freedom from powers outside ourselves and are blinded to the fact of inner restraints, compulsions, and fears, which tend to undermine the meaning of the victories freedom has

won against its traditional enemies. We therefore are prone to think that the problem of freedom is exclusively that of gaining still more freedom of the kind we have gained in the course of modern history, and to believe that the defence of freedom against such powers that deny such freedom is all that is necessary. We forget that, although each of the liberties which have been won must be defended with utmost vigour, the problem of freedom is not only a quantitative one, but a qualitative one; that we not only have to preserve and increase the traditional freedom, but that we have to gain a new kind of freedom, one which enables us to realize our own individual self; to have faith in this self and in life.[57]

5 Cross Connections

In this chapter we'll make cross connections throughout all the previous chapters. This means, that for instance phase 1 of the social development will be shown to be cross connected with phase 1 of the religious development. In this way the parallels that exist between the different developments will become visible. It will also become apparent that these phases are not isolated, but influence each other. The objective, process-oriented descriptions in the previous chapters will be abandoned to provide a more common, practical view of these developments. In doing so we can't avoid using a few historical examples that may be a bit coloured to some, if only because man is both subject and author of history and thus colours it simultaneously. Above all, however, the examples are meant to provide insight into the different developments. In following the course of the developments that have taken place in phases 1 and 2 we can even say something about phase 3, and the challenges and pitfalls that await us in the future.

5.1 Society

The process of social development can be roughly divided by the greatest changes in history: the rise of monotheism around 600 BC, the increase in prosperity since the Renaissance and the publication of the evolutionary theory by Darwin in the 19th century.[58] The following division, however, is viable also: the establishment of the sciences in Greece around 400 BC, the idea that religion is no longer absolute which led to the separation of church and state in the 16th century, and finally the destruction of every form of truth and validity during the Romantic Age at the end of the 18th century.[59] Of course, more moments in history can be singled out, which may serve as breaking points in time. In any case, the first phase always contains the natural system, after which in the second phase the social system is built up, and finally in the third phase the communicative process is followed through. As these phases build upon each other, they cannot take place in any different order. A social phase cannot be followed by a natural phase. On the other hand, in each phase of the process a society can be confronted with having to take a step backwards, for instance by an outbreak of war, or after a natural disaster. So much damage is done that a society is at least slowed down in its development, and it may take many years before the living standards rise up to the old level again.

The development of a society isn't necessarily influenced by external factors. An important internal factor is that the majority of the population finds itself in the same phase of development, and that in passing into a next phase the previous phase is largely closed by making clear agreements. If the conditions of the agreement aren't met in entering the next phase, elements of the previous phase will pop up again every once in a while until this previous phase is practically closed. We can find enough examples, from the past as well as the present, in which societies are already largely in phase 2 of their development, while phase 1 isn't quite completed. The chances are that physical violence, an element of the natural system, pops up again as soon as something in phase 2 happens that refers to an underlying feeling belonging to phase 1, which should have been dealt with before, such as harmful expressions or deeds in the area of religion, discrimination etc.

The incompatibilities between the different phases that co-exist in one and the same society will become clear in the following example. Person A is a publicist who is part of a democratic society which is in phase 2 of its development. In doing his job writing articles, he counts on the freedom of speech as an acquired right of the social system. Person B is part of the same society as person A, but by his deeply religious opinions he reasons with different ethics; from an ideological standpoint he actually finds himself at the end of phase 1 of the social development. Due to a publication by person A, which contains critical opinions on religions, person B works off his response as befits phase 1, by asserting his law of the right of the fittest. He will consider providing person A with a strong response, and perhaps even physically attack him, thereby supported by his opinions based on the rules that prevail in phase 1. Person C, also a member of this society and who also feels addressed by this publication, but who doesn't have a religious background, will respond in accordance with phase 2 of the social development. This person will counter the publicist with arguments, for example by seeking the media or holding him accountable in court. For persons B and C applies that they may gain their right by using the highest institutions of power, in the case of phase 2 being the court. This goes to show that when population groups find themselves in separate phases but must live together in the same cultural context, for instance because they reside within the same national boundaries, disputes may continue to arise in which one group responds vigorously to the other according to the rules of the developmental phase in which they respectively find themselves.

We also see the development of society resonated in the architectural constructions the human race has produced: from the first temples on isolated landmarks, the medieval church towers and castles, the campanile's in the Renaissance cities in Italy, the skyscrapers in North-America, the telecom masts which stand on top of them, to the communication satellites which orbit the earth. The mythical sanctuaries and church towers, which belong to phase 1, are replaced by the skyscrapers of the multinationals belonging to the economic development of phase 2, which in turn are topped by the cell phone masts and satellites that provide for communication in phase 3. This development shows that religion, as a central driving force behind human actions, must give way to the economic reality of the commercial market, which in turn is succeeded by the technical possibilities the means of communication afford. Of course, every step in this development answers to different needs: a characteristic of religion is an inner conviction, a social career results in a higher income, and the means of communication give us direct contact with our fellow men. Whether or not the one is better than the other is beside the point. It's about developments, and which consequences they have for the people that live within these circumstances. It's also important to add that when entering a next phase, the previous phase doesn't simply vanish into thin air. The culture of a society in part retains the acquired values and principles, traditions and rituals etc. within the new phase.

At the beginning of phase 2 of the social development there's a great difference between the incomes of the rich and the poor. The large industrial entrepreneurs clearly have higher incomes than the low paid assembly line workers. This difference in income is an automatic consequence of the growth of a capitalist society.

> The productivity of a modern economy cannot be achieved without the rational division of labor, and without creating winners and losers as capital shifts from one industry, region, or country to another.[60]

At a later stage the disadvantage employees have against the employer is more or less levelled out. The rights of the employees are extended: unions arise, as do minimum wages, the Factory Act, holiday allowance, etc. A consequence of these extended rights is that a company makes less profit, as more money goes to measures in favour of the employees, such as health contribution and pension build-up. When, at a given moment, the entrepreneur gains maximum production and the profits no longer grow, he must relocate his production line to low wage countries in order to 'make use' of the disadvantage in social provisions the employees in these countries have, thereby regaining profits using the same production methods. Until, of course, the rights and social provisions of those employees reach a higher level, and the company is yet again forced to relocate its production facility. In this way companies will travel the world, leaving a trail of prosperity. At the end of this process of equalisation by optimisation societies will emerge which are ready to take the step into phase 3.

A democratic and liberal society where citizens have equal rights, where there is no great difference in income, and where individual freedom is not held back in striving for optimal happiness, this is a society in which its citizens can feel most at home. Prosperity grows, and so does our life expectancy[61], and with more income our satisfaction of life grows as well.[62] The Scandinavian countries are those which for some time have been topping the charts of countries where people are the happiest about their lives.[63] For some time now the social level of these countries has maintained a certain status quo, enabling them to take the first step into phase 3 more readily. For instance, Finland is the first country in the world, which has determined that broad bandwidth data connections are every citizen's lawful right.[64]

Economically, of course, not everything will be completely optimised at the end of phase 2. The ingrained financial inequality effect from capitalism is undeniable. Apart from, for example, the differences in upbringing, the social circumstances, the presence or absence of physical limitations, the individual enrichment based on knowledge and skills remains. The trend towards the end of this phase, however, is that the differences diminish.

The present youth, which is so used to a high living standard, is of influence too, as they will less and less beware of the underlying class differences, or they will not experience them as disturbing or problematic. And, if we looked at the future from the past present we could perhaps hardly imagine the perspective of an optimised society. The early medieval citizen of a western country couldn't have suspected that a thousand years later the industrialisation (largely responsible for prosperity) and legislature (with equal rights guaranteed for all), to name two important influences, resulted in society as it exists today. The former differences which also determined the structure of society, namely that between the dictator and his subjects, between master and slave, between superior and inferior man, are almost completely levelled out at the end of the second phase.

In a society which finds itself at the beginning of phase 3, where the communicative and technological developments form two important ingredients, increasingly more is asked of the individual. In this phase everyone has become a manager of his own time, and a multitude of decisions must be made both on a professional and personal level. The individuals must communicate on their own on health services, municipalities, taxes, education facilities, children's day care, mortgages, insurances, bank accounts, job interviews, home care, etc. Given the excess of regulations and accompanying provisions, developed by the welfare state in phase 2, it becomes difficult for the individual to find the right counter in order to manage his provisions, let alone to make the right decisions based on an overkill of information. Additionally with large companies personal contact is difficult to make, because they will duly need to count on automated procedures themselves, to be more cost effective. The development of a technocracy, the dehumanisation of modern society, and the consequences that follow were already noted by Max Weber at the beginning of the 20th century:

> [...] Weber was at pains to point out that science could not provide values or tell us how to live; it could only provide new facts which might help us in our *decisions* about how to live. He thought that the most salient fact about the modern world is that it brings disenchantment. It is a world in which, he said, 'the gods neither have nor can have a home'. Modernity, for Weber, meant rationality, the organisation of affairs based on the trinity of efficiency, order and material satisfaction. This for him was achieved by means of legal, commercial and bureaucratic institutions that increasingly govern our relations with one another. The problem, as he saw it, was that commercial and industrial society, whatever freedoms and other benefits it has, brings disenchantment into our lives, eliminates any 'spiritual purpose' for mankind. He didn't think there was anything to be done about this; disenchantment was here to stay and had to be lived with.[65]

So an effect of this modern mass society, in which all is glorified and optimised, is the rise of a certain nihilism, a kind of worthlessness of the individual in comparison with his surrounding society. When all of society has reached personal freedom in this phase, then as a result, the binding elements are pressured. To what extent can we still speak of a society with shared values? If this isn't the case, then the society remains a jumble of individuals who all use their freedom to the utmost, as Riemen outlines:

> No longer is freedom -difficult and tragic freedom- the space that the individual needs to practice acquiring human dignity; rather, it is the *loss* of that dignity to the idolization of the animal ideal: everything is allowed. Meaning is unknown; sense is replaced with goal. "Fun" and "tasty" experiences replace the knowledge of good and evil. Because the everlasting doesn't exist, everything has to be now, new, and quick. No one can know any better, so everyone is right. Everyone is the same, so what is difficult is undemocratic. Art turns into entertainment, and what or whoever is famous is important. Gracián's statement that material weight determines the value of gold but moral weight determines human value is turned upside down. Morality? To each his own morality! Matter is king, and of all the little gods parading around, gold is the supreme deity. What is good for gold is good for you. Therefore be marketable! Adapt! Anything that makes you richer is useful, and what or who is not fun, not delightful, is in fact useless, can disappear. Everyone for himself, and no one for us all.[66]

Apart from the development of the individual during this phase, the changing economy also has an important role to play. A company will need to make more effort to deliver a qualitatively high grade product, more and better services, guarantee shorter delivery times, all this against a sharper price, and on a market where both local and international competition is high, the continuing technical developments being the greatest economic boost. Besides this, the new ways of communication between individuals in phase 3 also have an effect on the economy. Companies will increasingly sell and buy services using technological means. Marketing and image have become vitally important to the internationally operating companies. If only because, in the digital world, the consumers have an international platform at their disposal to enable them to voice their desires and complaints about all kinds of products or services. As soon as a society follows the path of economic and political freedom, it will not escape exchanging goods with other countries, thus making cultural exchanges as well. This process is currently tagged globalisation, as Fukuyama indicates:

> It is not the mark of provincialism but of cosmopolitanism to recognize that there has emerged in the last few centuries something like a true

global culture, centering around technologically driven economic growth and the capitalist social relations necessary to produce and sustain it.[67]

However, we can't say that the developments are only of a communicative or technological nature within a society that finds itself in phase 3. Aspects of the preceding phases 1 and 2 will keep playing their part, for example through a suppressing religion, greed and unequal treatment. However, just as the natural diversity of humans from phase 1 is socially equalised in phase 2, the economic inequality from phase 2 is more or less equalised in phase 3 within an open and ever accessible communicative society. In the second half of the developments in phase 3, the inequality between people will decrease. The independent, self-aware individual will then live in a society, which has been further optimised, and where self-development has become a central theme of action, and where aspects of phases 1 and 2 have fairly well become a thing of the past.

How can we position the current global developments in the processes described above? In which phase of social development have we arrived? Generally speaking, it isn't possible to indicate if 'world history' finds itself in phase 1, 2 or 3. It's more feasible to approach this per country, or perhaps per region, but still, most countries are a mix of phases 1, 2 and 3. No country can be pointed out to fully be in phase 2 or 3, thus having completely parted with phase 1. In view of industrialised countries, it is tempting to suppose that they represent modern society. However, 500 years ago people might have thought of this in the same way, and when in 500 years people look back at our time they will probably not jump to use the word 'modern' to signify our present society, since the way we live now will then have become hopelessly outdated.

With these considerations in mind we must be careful not to conclude that, when democratic elections have finally been held in a certain country, democracy may be anchored in it for good, and that this society can begin nourishing economic growth unhampered. A good foundation is of absolute importance, and necessary over a lengthy period of time in order not to let this country slide back into its former state without the democratic political establishment. Democracy was first formed in Greece, which however doesn't mean wars were not waged thereafter, or that since then every government that was formed endured the same measure of citizen involvement. In ancient Egypt the state provided for housing, women already had rights, and children received an education.[68] These are communal rights which in later times were partly revoked. Alternatively, once democracy is established, people can get used to it relatively quickly. Countries, that are now seen as modern -for example Spain, Portugal and Greece- still were military dictatorships in the 1970's. In keeping these details in the back of our minds, we can generally state that, despite the many set backs for instance due to a period of animosity and war, the social development of countries around the world can be seen to generally follow the same course, going from phase 1, through phase 2 to phase 3.

5.2 Politics

The most important political shift to take place is when man changes from the natural into the social phase. The dictator's power is then transferred to the whole population, which in turn can cause rivalry between individuals. The power of the dictator, which led to the suppression of the individuals, is removed, thus leading to individuals striving for power and/or status. The French philosopher Jean-Jacques Rousseau describes this transition from the natural into the social system:

> In proportion as ideas and sentiments succeed each other, and the head and the heart exercise themselves, men continue to shake off their original wildness, and their connections become more intimate and extensive. They now begin to assemble round a great tree: singing and dancing, the genuine offspring of love and leisure, become the amusement or rather the occupation of the men and women, free from care, thus gathered together. Every one begins to survey the rest, and wishes to be surveyed himself; and public esteem acquires a value. He who sings or dances best; the handsomest, the strongest, the most dexterous, the most eloquent, comes to be the most respected: this was the first step towards inequality, and at the same time towards vice. From these first preferences there proceeded on one side vanity and contempt, on the other envy and shame; and the fermentation raised by these new leavens at length produced combinations fatal to happiness and innocence.[69]

Liberalism, capitalism and democracy are the elements that make the transition to phase 2 happen in this process.

The incentive to capitalism is the competition between men, based on certain talent, skill or knowledge, resulting in an increase in possessions. The hunger for power, possession and position now lies with the individual, a situation which closely corresponds with the beginnings of phase 1, where the natural right of the fittest was the determining factor. In most cases the success of one's endeavours is measured by the amount of material possessions or acknowledgement one gains. More acknowledgement from one's surroundings is a boost for one's ego, as it affirms the individual's rising status in the ranking order of mutual competition. In part three we will further describe the role the so-called iconic hero plays in the endeavour for success. A set of rules is necessary to control the competition among men, otherwise we would be stepping back into the natural phase. In a democracy everyone is equal before the law. An important step in this process is that the 'natural' power of the individual is transferred to the state, and the thus established government provides for the safekeeping of the individual from lapsing back into phase 1. In taking this step, it is important for the legal system that the public involvement is retained in it. This is one of the most important conditions to arrive at phase 2.

Closely linked to the process, where a population turns to democracy, is that with it a path is also made clear for liberalism. Democracy ensures that every individual has equal possibilities for involvement in the policies executed by the chosen government. In principle everyone is heard and everyone is equal in making themselves heard. If all the individuals of a society can refer to having equal rights, can be obliged to perform equal duties, and are free to do as they please within this law, then the basic principles have been laid out for a liberal society.

However the transition from phase 1 to phase 2, especially in the beginning, not only provides advantages. Societies, that find themselves in phase 2 of their development and are based on a combination of democracy, liberalism and capitalism, will inherently be faced with a specific aspect of capitalism, namely that it contributes to financial inequality. The differences between individuals are made, and financially enhanced, based on talent or appreciation. If you are the best at the 100 meter sprint, if you are selected Miss Universe, if you are the best at moving the audience, in the theatre or on screen, then *you* are the exception to the rule, then *you* are a hero, and the fame and matching rewards will come your way. An additional consequence of this individual development is that we can all become 'heroes', and thus gain a measure of individual acknowledgement and self-respect, an aspect to which we will return later in part three. The best known example of this is of course North America: the New World proverb is that everyone can make their dream come true, which actually defines the United States as the apex of liberalism and capitalism. The 'individual pursuit of happiness' even has a prominent place in the American Declaration of Independence. A disadvantage of the individual appreciation is that not everyone is as enterprising, talented, smart or beautiful, which results in financial inequality, thus richer and poorer people. In a socially functioning system the financial differences are more or less levelled out by the tax system: the broadest shoulders must bear the heaviest burdens.

The solidarity between individuals in an open, liberal society is another subject of attention. In such an open society everyone can develop himself: the population is diverse and it exists of the erudite as well as the simpleton. But why would one individual put his life on the line to defend another individual in an armed conflict? There is a real possibility that a society will emerge consisting of people living *along side* each other, but not *with* each other, because they don't embrace a common spirit or cause. A more ethical argument against this process is that in a later phase, and in combination with capitalism, the population will develop into a society consisting of disinterested, selfish individuals, who only strive for self-enrichment mainly of material possessions. Because eventually, the social success, the social status, is measured by one's possessions, the rewards for hard work.

Beside the financial inequality, that arises through capitalism, there is a counterforce which by and by emerges from the same system. At the moment when a situation arises in which every country in the world finds itself at the end of phase 2 of the social development, then the capitalist system will arrive at an unusual situation. The international companies' approach to manufacture products in low wage countries in order to guarantee profit margins will no longer work, as there will be no more low wage countries left. The welfare level will have risen, even in the low wage countries, due to the local multinational production facilities. Apart from the ever present necessity to innovate, how can these multinationals keep making a profit? This sets in motion global equalisation, in general prosperity as well as in the profit margins of the multinational companies.

> Caught up in day-to-day events, it is easy to forget that a longer view reveals an almost unstoppable historical trend towards greater equality. It runs like a river of human progress from the first constitutional limitations on the 'divine' (and arbitrary) right of kings, and continues on through the slow development of democracy and the establishment

of the principle of equality before the law. It swells with the abolition of slavery and is strengthened by the extension of the franchise to include non-property-owners and women. It picks up pace with the development of free education, health services and systems of minimum income maintenance covering periods of unemployment and sickness. It runs on to include legislation to protect the rights of employees and tenants, and legislation to prevent racial discrimination. It includes the decline of forms of class deference. The abolition of capital and corporal punishment is also part of it. So too is the growing agitation for greater equality of opportunity - regardless of race, class, gender, sexual orientation and religion. We see it also in the increasing attention paid by lobby groups, social research and government statistical agencies to poverty and inequality over the last fifty years; and most recently we see it in the attempt to create a culture of mutual respect.[70]

Economically, this equalisation isn't very good for the companies' profit margins, but positive for the human societies. It appears that in a society, where the differences between the highest and lowest incomes are the least, the population has a longer life expectancy and less newborn mortality, crime and other social problems.[71]

As for the political process, the transition from phase 2 to phase 3 is much more evident than from phase 1 to phase 2. Capitalism harbours a deep rooted motivation which lies at the heart of every individual. One individual wants to be better, faster, stronger, more esteemed and have more possessions than another. However, at the end of phase 2 in the social development a situation arises where this difference between individuals in various areas has become negligible. At the beginning of phase 3 everyone has equal rights and duties, and for the most part the same value of possessions. Economically, politically and socially, everyone is treated in the same way, every person has access to the same social provisions, etc. The inequality, that capitalism caused at the beginning of phase 2 will then largely be annulled. This would amount to a very socially balanced society. But, then the motivation ensuring that one would want to be better than the other, wouldn't exist in this scenario. The competitive feelings in phase 2 have always led to extraordinary sports achievements, astounding art, moving music and all kinds of innovative industrial achievements, that make life more agreeable. With century upon century of striving and urging in our genes, at the close of phase 2 of the social development, the very social behaviour and the collective equalisation defining phase 3 seem a more difficult hurdle to take than we can currently imagine.

In phase 3 as well, mutual competition will remain, although it will rather be focussed on the personal infill, a strive for self-realisation. This can be a creative expression, a sports achievement or an important scientific discovery or technological invention. The mutual competition in this phase will not so much be aimed at acquiring possessions, but it will rather be focussed on sharing the achievements with others. Whereby the technical resources, such as mobile phones, and the internet, will play a large facilitating role.

In this phase, where technocracy is the political system, the structure of different political parties has become obsolete. This political structure from phase 2 is based on representatives of the people nurturing certain interests. Where there are different population groups different interests must be served. At the end of phase 2 this situation has changed for the whole population due to optimised equalisation. The sole remaining interest to be served now is that of everyone. By consequence, the political differentiation between population groups becomes redundant. Technocracy and globalisation come together in the following quote:

> The post-historical world would still be divided into nation-states, but its separate nationalisms would have made peace with liberalism and would express themselves increasingly in the sphere of private life alone. Economic rationality, in the meantime, will erode many traditional features of sovereignty as it unifies markets and production.[72]

The environment in which this system already functions is the Internet. Many companies in the world work on computer programmes which they distribute free of charge. These programmes are better known as freeware or open source software. Ever since the Internet became open to the public, it has been possible to set up a communications channel, thereby surpassing the traditional national borders, and to produce a product through global collaboration for which the customer, eventually, need not pay a thing. The developers satisfy themselves with certain acknowledgement, based on how many times the product is downloaded, and the user often only sees a short on-screen advertisement.

The political system and its matching economic system, in the technocracy of phase 3, must take into account a society which increasingly focusses on technological development and digital communication. It no longer matters where people are located. Basically they always have access to their own digital files, and can communicate at any given time with other individuals around the world. A clear disadvantage of this is when we don't have our personal digital assistant at hand, we can't get home without our navigation system, nor be able to immediately call our friends to ask for help, and in time perhaps can't even do our mental maths. Our dependence on technologies in this phase is evident, especially when our most important data will also be stored on one all-encompassing carrier. Will we soon only be identified by an id card? Our privacy could thus become rather pressured in this technocracy. The commercial companies are already gathering as much personal information as possible to sell their products to customers as best and as often as they can. By combining the various kinds of information, the data on our mobile phone, e-mails, mouse clicks on a website, filled out enquiries, concert attendants, subscriptions to clubs etc., these become a map of our individual behaviour, of our individual spending pattern. This information is stored in market research, databases for consumer data, PR or spending patterns. We could start to feel like being a blockbusting celebrity: everything we do, everywhere we've been, is registered and can at any given time be checked by someone else. This might not seem like a problem at present, but this can change when that explicit response to a blog, or that not so charming picture from a party pops up in a job interview. Our digital tracks then prove to be irreversible. Giving up our privacy seems the price we must pay as individuals in this increasingly data rich society. Although, groups of individuals are already offering resistance to such breaches of privacy. A possible consequence is that, when the freedom of the individuals begins to form too great a threat for the ruling political leaders, who in spite of it wish to keep control over the political system and maintain the power that comes with it, the over-regulating technocracy will change into a police state. This could be a key question for a future technocracy: will the individual have the freedom to control his or her own life, or will the government practice far-reaching control to keep the 'free' individuals in check?

The future of politics is of course difficult to foretell, but it may be highly unlikely for a society in phase 2 to take a step back into the dictatorship of phase 1, as prosperity has already well penetrated the different levels of society, and the individuals are enabled to appeal to all kinds of rights encompassed in common laws. This of course doesn't rule out undetermined external factors, such as natural disasters, which can cause great poverty and can lead a nation to lapse back into phase 1. For a society, which already shows characteristics of phase 3, the use of computers, mobile phones and the internet has become so commonplace, that the effects these technical possibilities will have on us will only increase. Given the greater role of global communication, the local or national politics could become less important. And, to us individuals it will become clear that we all reside on the same planet and should learn to cooperate with each other. A society which is in an advanced stage in phase 3 will have less difficulty with this approach, the natural system of phase 1 with its internal rivalries will then be an actual thing of the past.

5.3 Religion

Science and religion are often seen as two opposing movements. Both are based on a method in which reality is described as some form of truth. A religion does this by placing the source of everything within the godly or the elusive realm, based on written sources or oral tradition. These texts are subject to interpretation and can therefore be defined as subjective descriptions of reality. The natural sciences try to describe reality by searching for the source of everything in the characteristics of nature, and drafting explanations by combining research results. The results of a study or an experiment must always and everywhere be replicable, cannot be interpreted otherwise, and must be presented objectively. The equal sign, as we saw in the chapter Nothing is Lost, is of the utmost importance here.

For the religious as well as the scientific explanation of the world, the result of both efforts will always be that they are approaches to reality. Both use their own methods and symbols to explain reality. Reality itself is omnipresent. It is what it is, it is objective. Human observation is not needed for reality to exist. The truth, however, is an interpretation of the objective reality, and it is dependent on for instance the sensory possibilities of the observer, resulting in a subjective truth. We are generally inclined to think that there is no difference between reality and truth. This, however, only happens because of the way reality presents itself to us, and thus corresponds with our subjective truth. According to philosophers Galileo Galilei and John Locke certain characteristics of objects, like colour, taste and smell, are dependent on the person observing the object.[73] The German philosopher Immanuel Kant argued that we could never grasp the real characteristics of an object, the 'thing itself', as what we observe is always some form of truth, our own interpretation of reality.[74]

Truth being an approach to reality is evident also when new facts are presented, that for instance influence a certain religion. When archaeologists find fossil remains of dinosaurs and this discovery doesn't coincide with the truth this religion maintains, this fact is denied, saying e.g. 'the earth is only 6000 years old, these fossil remains can't be that old, so they must be fake'. Or the fact is thus interpreted and explained that it does fit in with the doctrine of this religion, saying e.g. 'God put these remains in the earth himself'. For the natural sciences these discoveries are a source of information, providing inspiration to do further research, or enabling to adapt current ideas about the animal lineage to arrive at a better explanation for it. In this example, religion upholds a subjective truth, whereas the sciences strive for an objective truth. Both approach reality, but within each approach reality remains beyond reach.

While the knowledge of the world around us increases on the basis of scientific efforts, what role could there be left for religion or for the divine? As we become ever more knowledgeable of our surroundings by being able to explain more of our world, the number of aspects we could ascribe to the divine decrease. Lightning has been explained by meteorologist as a discharge of electricity between the atmosphere and the earth, a clear example of cause and effect. The natural phenomenon occurs separate from our intentions, or negligences towards the gods. We can even let it happen in a lab. The influence of this phenomenon, formerly ascribed to the gods, is now described and explained by science. When placed in the sequel of developmental phases, the religious aspects that belonged to phase 1 are now explained by science in phase 2 of the social development. The increase in knowledge largely demystifies the human world view which was established in phase 1. Science has, of course, not only had an influence on the religious sphere. In the last centuries many developments took place, e.g. in the realms of medicine, industrial processes, and agriculture, which brought great wealth to countries that had arrived at phase 2.[75]

Imagine the time when science is able to explain everything, that everything has been charted, and that we have total control over our bodies and the world. We will never become ill again, we'll have gained eternal life, society will be fully optimised, etc. Through science we would reach the point where most religions also arrive at, namely a perfect world in which everything is good, beautiful and peaceful, a heaven on earth. As such, the paths taken by religion and science are different, but they lead to the same result.

However, the likelihood that we can understand our environment completely, is very small. We will never be able to know, research or explain everything. Inexplicable things will always remain, even only because some things simply are difficult to study. For astronomers some planets are simply too far away, and in the field of history the subject of study takes place in the past. For this reason a religion, and generally, a philosophy of life, will always remain the domain of the inexplicable, the subjective, the mysterious. In these voids of our knowledge, the unknowable, unfathomable terrain, the belief in a god or the divine will live on. As the French philosopher Voltaire described the function of god: 'If God hadn't existed, it would have been necessary to invent Him.'[76] The natural sciences, on the other hand, are best at objectively describing our world, the hard facts, the verifiable research data. Both visions on reality are best in their own arenas, they mustn't go fishing in each others ponds, for neither would catch anything.

Biologist Stephen Jay Gould pleaded for the segregation of natural sciences and religion. He proposed not to debate the scientific facts on religious grounds, and vice versa, but to keep them strictly separated. These two distinguishing fields, or magisteria as Gould called them, should keep off each others terrain, which he signified with NOMA, Non-Overlapping Magisteria:

> For example, if you believe that an adequately loving God must show his hand by peppering nature with palpable miracles, or that such a God could only allow evolution to work in a manner contrary to facts of the fossil record (as a story of slow and steady linear progress toward *Homo sapiens*, for example), then a particular, partisan (and minority) view of religion has transgressed into the magisterium of science by dictating conclusions that must remain open to empirical test and potential rejection. Similarly, to the scientist who thinks that he has gained the right to determine the benefits and uses of a new and socially transforming invention merely because he made the potentiating discovery and knows more than anyone else about the technical details -and who resents the moral concerns of well-informed citizens, especially their insistence upon some role in a dialogue about potential regulation- NOMA answers with equal force that facts of nature cannot determine the moral basis of utility, and that a scientist has no more right to seek such power than his fundamentalist neighbor can muster in trying to become dictator of the age of the earth.[77]

But, it isn't easy to strictly separate these two magisteria. The sciences actually do explain matters formerly attributed to religion and thus deemed inexplicable, we only need to refer to the example of lightning already discussed. Today, hardly anyone would still believe this to be the gods' bad omen.

Most of us know now that this is a meteorological phenomenon. The former subjective interpretation of this phenomenon by religion is exchanged for the objective description by the natural sciences. Science has gained more credibility on this subject than the belief in a god, which by the way resulted in a remarkable street scenery these days where all the church towers are fitted with lightning conductors. So, there actually is an overlap in Magisteria or better, a transfer of the phenomenon from one magisterium to the other. Alternatively, one can say that lightning has become explicable just *because* it is a natural phenomenon, which occurs under certain circumstances and thus becomes measurable, available for research, and under certain circumstances replicable in a lab setting. From the scientific point of view, this might be a satisfactory solution, but for the subjective species we humans are, it isn't the only one. We need hope, faith, motivation, consolation, conviction and various other 'soft' human principles and values, that can't be explained by the exact sciences. We need to assign these principles and values, as the emotional creatures we are, to situations or persons in order to live together. In other words, life is much more about knowing how to live with each other, than to gain precise answers as to how life actually works. And it is questionable whether everything that is identified with a god or the divine will ever be accurately understood by the sciences. What's more, as in religion, the sciences work with a basic set of presumptions, which also provoke contradictions.[78] The present scientific explanation of the beginnings of the universe are based on the Big Bang theory. We can't explain what happened before that, as space and time, as we understand today, didn't exist then, the universe was in a state of singularity. However, the ever increasing pressure and enormous energy build-up led to an expansion of matter, and suddenly there was space-time. This does sound very unreal, rather like a miracle. With a little imagination you could call it a *creatio ex nihilo*.

Perhaps it's better to explain the difference between science and religion in another way, for example that the sciences are more about the quantity of life, and the philosophies of life are more about the quality of life. The sciences answer questions like: what is life? What is it made of? How does it function? The answers are specifically found in biology and genetics, and in the natural sciences in general. But the philosophies of life are concerned with answering questions like: how should we live? What do we value in this life? Traditionally we tend to find answers to these questions in the areas of philosophy, ethics and religion.

The establishment of religions took place in phase 1 of the social development. With the disappearance of the ancient cultures of e.g. Egypt and Greece, the gods and the accompanying rituals have faded into the background as well. Religion has become less important for individuals in a society at the end of phase 2 of the social development. In materialistic terms they and their social surroundings are well off. The increase in wealth and knowledge in phase 2 means a decided decrease in religious influence on society. The churches and temples will mostly be filled in times of disaster or need, a process that fits with a temporary setback into phase 1. This emphasises one important function of religion, which is the hope for better times and the consolation found in it. The religious movements, which come about in phase 2 of the social development, focus more on broader opinions, which should rather be seen as philosophies of life than as preachings of a new world religion.

In phase 3 of the social development no religions will be established resembling those rooted in phase 1, as this has long since become past history. These 'old' religions, their source being close to nature and with mostly an external, inexplicable divine entity, actually no longer fit in with the developments that take place in this phase. A society in phase 3 consists mostly of people who strive for self-realisation, where the motivation to discover one's self-consciousness is foremost an internal quest. This doesn't mean that the old religions are completely discarded. Adapting the old religions to this new situation in using the personal infill provides them with a new sense of validity.

5.4 The individual

The industrial developments in phase 2 of the social development are of great importance to the individual. Due to economic and technological progress the unique hand-made products from phase 1 are replaced by products made in factories using standardised production processes. Over time, less and less people are needed in these factories, often only for maintenance or to keep an eye on the machines that are preprogrammed to do all the hard labour. By automating the production process further and further the costs have much decreased. At a certain moment the product can't be made cheaper. The price of resources is at its lowest point, the margins by which to improve the product become smaller and smaller, while the costs for these marginal improvements become higher and higher. Companies must then increasingly deploy marketing, service and customer satisfaction to sell the same amount of products. But, here too, in order to cut costs and maximise profits the customer services are standardised, and the individual as a customer can become the victim. Customer requests outside the fixed plan, to the manufacturer or the government official for instance, can no longer be sufficiently answered or take up too much time to follow up on. The whole consumer society runs on this mechanism of the standardisation of large scale production. The specific repair of an already rather cheaply produced product just costs too much, which means it's simply cheaper to buy a new one. In this consumer society there's one big loser, namely the environment, since all the broken down and used products end up here. It should be clear that by proceeding in this manner we are exhausting our natural living environment. We use the natural resources to transform them into products that we want, and when we no longer need them, we discard them back into nature where they lay in waste.

In phase 2 of the individual development the liberal, capitalist society has an important influence on the behaviour of each individual. Due to the structure of this society, the individual is forced to present himself like a commodity on the market, as Fromm puts it:

> His body, his mind and his soul are his capital, and his task in life is to invest it favorably, to make a profit of himself. Human qualities like friendliness, courtesy, kindness, are transformed into commodities, into assets of the "personality package," conducive to a higher price on the personality market. If the individual fails in a profitable investment of himself, he feels that *he* is a failure; if he succeeds, *he* is a success. Clearly, his sense of his own value always depends on factors extraneous to himself, on the fickle judgment of the market, which decides about his value as it decides about the value of commodities. He, like all commodities that cannot be sold profitably on the market, is worthless as far as his exchange value is concerned, even though his use value may be considerable.[79]

By the process of equalisation through optimisation at the end of phase 2 of the social development the differences between individuals in various domains are almost completely levelled out. At the beginning of phase 3 this is an achievement of each individual. But if all are largely equal, the question arises: does the individual still gain the personal acknowledgement he so longs for? Haven't we all become rather ordinary?

The American artist Andy Warhol once said, that in the future everyone will have 15 minutes of fame.[80] At the beginning of phase 3, the communicative phase, it might rather be 15 seconds of shame that we might claim. For, in the communicative phase we continuously have a limitless number of platforms at our disposal to publish whatever we want. We can all become actors, authors, cameramen and directors, without there being any necessity for a message or an idea at the base of it, and without having the product scrutinised by a critic. Our own interest or presence is good enough, we are our own arbiter. We claim the moment because *we* decide what will happen, we don't depend on others, we don't need to earn it. Fleetingness, sensation, excitement, these are the most important ingredients, and as a result the attention span of the receiver of the message might not even be as long as 15 seconds, given the abundance of the material. By consequence, in this phase there is a stronger appeal to the individual's capacity for self-reflection. The self-correcting attitude of the traditional groups from phase 2 in the social development, which is based on a segregation by religion, union, club or political party, is no longer strong enough in this third phase to influence the individual on the point of religion, politics and social characteristics. As a result, the individual no longer feels ashamed of anything. Without self-reflection or the correctness of one's peers the individual could eventually alienate from society.

In addition, the individual develops an increasing distance in dealing with work-related matters. The development from skills and craftsmanship in phase 1 up to the industrialised work in phase 2 has made certain that workers are seeing less and less of what they ultimately produce. Instead of making a sword or some tapestry from start to finish, they now become spokes in a wheel, responsible for just one part of a whole, not aware of the final product at the end of the production line. As professions have become highly specialised, it is difficult to maintain a good overview: the involvement with the work, in the sense of having joint responsibility for the final product, is difficult to maintain for the average worker.

> Two centuries ago, our forebears would have known the precise history and origin of nearly every one of the limited number of things they ate and owned, as well as of the people and tools involved in their production. They were acquainted with the pig, the carpenter, the weaver, the loom and the dairymaid. The range of items available for purchase may have grown exponentially since then, but our understanding of their genesis has diminished almost to the point of obscurity. We are now as imaginatively disconnected from the manufacture and distribution of our goods as we are practically in reach of them, a process of

alienation which has stripped us of myriad opportunities for wonder, gratitude and guilt.[81]

The alienation from the world, in private as in business, may lead to a complete apathetic response to whatever stimulus, being overfed by all the media-babble, and deprived of real personal recognition and appreciation. With the additional development of a technocratic society, where the individual will feel less appreciated as a person than he is identified via ID card or online status, the future central position of the individual is at stake. In the second part of phase 3 there will be a shift in this process. The decadence of material prosperity, pursuing easy online acknowledgement, fleeing into all kinds of consumptive behaviour, and the simple and quick satisfaction of every whim, will become a burden. In the second part of phase 3 all conditions for the former phases are met and man is living in the most optimised world. This is the best moment for the individual to gain personal recognition and development, and to leave that individual fingerprint on human history. It is now possible for the individual to do what he actually wants to do and what suits his nature best. And so, the individual creeps out from under the blanket of peer behaviour which was such a defining factor in phase 2, and does what he is most drawn to at that given moment. This will be another difficult step. As in every phase transition is marked by some kind of revolution: this time not on a societal and political level, such as the transition from phase 1 to 2, but rather on a personal level. Every individual will have to determine this for himself. He must take this step by himself. Only then will true self-realisation take place. A society will develop, in which individuals do what they really want, knowing what they're capable of, who are really driven, who truly develop themselves in different areas. The self-realisation of the individual requires a more introspective approach. By acceptance and self-analysis the recognition of the individual at last becomes the central point.

This doesn't mean that society will exist of individuals who operate independently and no longer maintain contact with other people. This is the point where all boundaries between individuals fall away, where making contact becomes ever easier and contacts become richer. Social contacts have as great an impact on our lives as do smoking, obesity or high blood pressure. A lonely person currently has twice the risk of dying as a person with a rich social life.[82] In this phase, not the most hansom, the richest, smartest or most successful people, but the most socially skilled people will also be the happiest. And, these social contacts are much needed, since it's no longer the consuming customers from phase 2, but rather the creative people who need to exert themselves in this phase. In phase 3 the adage is an adaptation of the phrase 'to publish or to perish', what now holds true for everyone is 'to create or to consume' or 'to create or not to create'. Either you produce something of your own, or you consume something produced by someone else.

As opposed to the start of phase 3 the individual will need to break with his comfortable situation. He'll have to free himself of the taste and generalist opinions of the masses to clearly shape his own identity. The individual must become more aware of his own possibilities, thoughts and preferences. Fromm describes this transition, this break away from the group, as follows:

> Conscience, by its very nature is nonconforming; it must be able to say no, when everybody else says yes; in order to say this "no" it must be certain in the rightness of the judgement on which the no is based. To the degree to which a person conforms he cannot hear the voice of his conscience, much less act upon it. Conscience exists only when man experiences himself as man, not as a thing, as a commodity.[83]

Over the centuries the individual is slowly climbing up the ladder to self-realisation. In summary we can say, that phase 1, that of having blind faith in a religion or dictator, passes into phase 2, emphasising on knowledge led by science and an economy driven by technological developments, and ends in phase 3 with the self-realisation of the individual. The individual progresses from the natural system, through science and the social system, to a situation in which the focus lies on the complete self-realisation of the individual.[84] During this process, which may stretch over a period of thousands of years, an unparalleled shift will take place in knowledge, power and responsibility.

In this part we discussed the most important processes of the social, political and religious developments and that of the individual. How the individual communicates with the world around him and which specific implications this has for the him will be tackled in part three.

PART III

MAN

Introduction

In part one we discussed The One Self, The Antagonists, Nothing is Lost and Singularity as the basic building blocks of the Concatenator. We already saw that the core aspect of The One Self is self-preservation: it will do all it can to survive by using power to gain control over the current situation and by limiting as much as possible the loss of that control, which would otherwise lead to fear.

In part three we will focus further on power and fear, the two antagonists influencing The One Self. We will see that The One Self has different methods at it's disposal to cope with the hard realities of daily life. Man tries to gain control over specific circumstances and generally over his own life, by visualising himself in the role of a hero who rises above reality. The individual maintains this ideal to turn away from his greatest fear, that of death, because it threatens the core aspect of his existence, his self-preservation. By attaching value to the world around him and by gaining acknowledgement and reward for his deeds, the individual tries to create a world valid to himself. Once again, at the end of this part we will make cross connections between all preceding chapters by using examples from daily practice.

1 Conscience

Let's say you're walking along the beach, hand-in-hand with your girlfriend, a light breeze is blowing from the sea caressing your face. In the distance the silhouette of a ship draws up against the sun setting along the horizon. All around you hear the cry of seagulls.

Suddenly, the thought comes to mind that at a given moment you will no longer experience this event, you realise that it is short-lived. Inevitably you will die at a certain moment, and then all this will be over. So at the end of this beautiful summer's day you are suddenly confronted with your own mortality.

The reason for this sudden contemplation of our own situation, is that we have a conscience. We are aware of our current situation, but also of our past thoughts and deeds, and our future plans and wishes. How best to describe conscience, and where it can be found in our body, has for centuries been food for thought for philosophers, psychologists, and man in general.[1, 2] It's not the objective here to provide an all-encompassing description of conscience, but it at least contains aspects such as observing the surroundings and the power to respond to it, memorising experiences and being able to resort to them according to the situation, and a certain ability of coordination to be in command of the organism. In any case, the most important thing for the organism is to strive for the continued existence of The One Self by responding to what is happening in the immediate surroundings. For then, the organism becomes aware of the necessity for self-preservation. When defining conscience in this way, it follows that animals and plants have a conscience. They respond to their environment, they adapt themselves when there is less food, they possess an attack or defence mechanism to protect their organism, they build territories and procreate. This of course applies differently for every organism, and possibly isn't as complex as we find in humans. But, perhaps other animals and plants have different forms of conscience, yet unknown to us.[3]

As far as humans are concerned, we can at least say that, we are aware of our surroundings via our senses, and that these surroundings present themselves to us as matters of fact all the time. For instance, when someone stands on our foot, we feel it (by nerve impulses in our foot) and we experience it as something painful (by registering these nerve impulses in our brains, linking them with our conscience), because it is our own foot (the reality of our own body), not someone else's (no imagined emotion), we're not dreaming (we don't awaken with a fright) and we can remember it later (by memorising it, for example, as an emotion).

As beings on this earth, we are part of nature, we originate from it; we are animals with insight. Because of this insight we are not just a typical animal solely acting on impulses. This insight contains all kinds of elements: being able to self-reflect, making plans for the future, or looking back on the past to deeds done of which we now feel sorrow or remorse, reflecting on moral issues or on life after death. This gives us the possibility to communicate in detail, to pass on information to a next generation even after we've gone. By our own conscience, we are fully aware of our own mortality. This confrontation with hard facts also gives us a special place in the universe.

> By being aware of himself as distinct from nature and other people, by being aware -even very dimly-of death, sickness, ageing, he necessarily feels his insignificance and smallness in comparison with the universe and all others who are not "he".[4]

Death is our greatest fear, and so self-preservation, the control of ourselves and avoiding fear are our most important goals, as we have seen in part one. Or, as Becker articulates the human situation and his final destiny:

> What does it mean to be a *self-conscious animal*? The idea is ludicrous, if it is not monstrous. It means to know that one is food for worms. This is the terror: to have emerged from nothing, to have a name, consciousness of self, deep inner feelings, an excruciating inner yearning for life and self-expression and with all this yet to die.[5]

The confrontation with death can arise at any given moment, which is a life threatening situation, as this concerns the very end of the individual. We all know that death is an absolute certainty of life. By our own conscience we experience this horrifying thought as a real confrontation. Following, we will want to protect ourselves against this inevitable fact.

2 Hero

We can all play the role of the hero. The hero may be a politician, a sportsman, artist or scientist, but also, our neighbour doing a good deed. A hero is someone who by his actions or thoughts, for him or for others, achieves a moment of invincibility, and thereby draws attention to himself. The hero has a hard task ahead of him, but follows through nonetheless. Though he may disregard other people's good advice, he has an inner motivation which makes him exceed the commonplace. It gives him the opportunity to follow his own course, making the impossible possible. He stands the hard test with apparent ease and eventually triumphs over the invincible, if only for an instant.

A hero is someone who was or is of historical importance to a certain group of people, one who has left important writings, won a battle, made an important discovery, invented a medicine against a dangerous disease, saved someone from death by drowning, etc. The people reward this hero with a statue, a street name, a national celebration day, an article in the local newspaper, or in some other way, in order to commemorate time and again how special this person was for the town or nation. In this way, the hero lives on in our collective memories, he 'outlives' so to speak his own time by not being forgotten. Thus, the hero is the perfect personification of our way of overcoming our mortality, our subconscious, natural and intuitive fear of death. By his deeds, the hero becomes the personification of the myth: at the moment of his heroic deed he has total control over a situation.

> The myth is a way of expressing the conception that the world and the powers that reign are not left at the mercy of utter whim. Which ever way the myth is presented in the social world, albeit by dividing the powers or by regulating mutual relationships, the myth is always about cancelling out the notion of arbitrariness.[6]

We come across heroes everywhere and in different cultures, from early legends, myths and tales, until the modern films, books, comics and video

games. Through oral tradition we are still familiar with the heroes of yester-
year and of their roles in history. From the hero's point of view, however,
the people's acknowledgement of him mustn't go too far. We all want recognition, but no one wants to be recognised. It would be an invasion of the
hero's privacy. Our hero would become too exposed to the outside world,
which could be at the expense of his recognition. This aspect of being a
public figure is often called 'the price of being famous'.

> It doesn't matter whether the cultural hero-system is frankly magical,
> religious, and primitive or secular, scientific, and civilized. It is still a
> mythical hero-system in which people serve in order to earn a feeling
> of primary value, of cosmic specialness, of ultimate usefulness to crea-
> tion, of unshakable meaning. They earn this feeling by carving out
> a place in nature, by building an edifice that reflects human value: a
> temple, a cathedral, a totem pole, a skyscraper, a family that spans three
> generations. The hope and belief is that the things that man creates in
> society are of lasting worth and meaning, that they outlive or outshine
> death and decay, that man and his products count.[7]

It should be clear that the hero is a leader, someone who charts a course,
who has a certain idea and acts upon it, who is an example to everyone, and
creates a bond between people. The people who are inspired by the opinions
of the leader are the followers; as to a chief commander this is the army, as to
a sports person it is the supporters, and to a pop idol it's the fans. The danger
in this is of course that the follower doesn't criticise the hero, and doesn't
accept criticism from others regarding this hero. The follower will blindly
keep following the course the hero has set out. This idolisation is relatively
innocent in the light of a pop idol. However, regarding a charismatic leader
of a large army, this can have far reaching consequences.
Most people though, are no heroes: they have done no heroic deeds nor
have special ideas rewarding them a leading role; they are not the exception
to the rule. Instead, every individual can take refuge, for instance to group
behaviour and put on a football shirt, thus identifying themselves with the
club hero playing on the field. In social psychology this type of behaviour
is called 'basking in reflected glory'. It is a simple but effective method to
reflect the glory of our hero upon ourselves, thereby boosting our own ego,
which also has a positive effect on The One Self. Without being able to play
football ourselves, and just by watching it and wearing the club T-shirt, the
victory of the football team becomes a victory that reflects on us as well.

Or perhaps, we will want to do something outrageous. If we practice hard enough, there's a chance that we'll be included in the Guinness Book of Records, the modern-day book of heroes. These days there's hardly any honour in being a global explorer. There's more honour to gain from discoveries in the minute by studying the atoms, or the immense by studying the cosmic world. Due to their highly specialist nature, these fields of research are mostly inaccessible to the average citizen.

In short: as heroes, we want to receive recognition from our fellow man, the day-to-day infill can easily be translated into a measure of popularity we receive. The more attention drawn to us as the hero, the more important we seem to be.

> The self-confidence, the "feeling of self", is merely an indication of what others think of the person. It is not he who is convinced of his value regardless of popularity and his success on the market. If he is sought after, he is somebody; if he is not popular, he is simply nobody. This dependence of self-esteem on the success of the "personality" is the reason why for modern man popularity has this tremendous importance. On it depends not only whether or not one goes ahead in practical matters, but also whether one can keep up one's self-esteem or whether one falls into the abyss of inferiority feelings.[8]

The degree of his popularity is a common measure for the hero. It becomes more difficult to establish popularity in someone of no national repute. But still, here too the heroic role is necessary, however trivial the deed. We can't all be the first on Mount Everest, nor be the first to set foot on the moon. We do small deeds on a local scale, we create things, for the ones we care about, for some acknowledgement by our family and friends, and we hope for glory and recognition in our own social circles.

The hero remains a projection of human mortality, and perhaps just an added confirmation of it, despite his powers of healing or uniting a group of people. They cling to an image of the past, which is often too romanticised. To the hero, however, life is no unending feast. But, this is a role most people never play, as they are often mere participants in their own lives. They don't know who is directing the show, and they'll gradually disappear offstage while the applause dies away. However, just like the average mortal soul, at a certain moment the hero will die as well, often heroically of course. Nevertheless, it doesn't take away the fact that even the hero, just like everyone else, is subject to the laws of the world.

3 The Neurotic Types

We are all aware of our mortality - even the hero will (physically) die at some point in time. Our fear of death, our incapacity to cope with the disappearance of The One Self, is in odds with our consciousness, our control of The One Self. It's a battle of the irrational world, the world of arbitrariness, against that of the rational individual who wants to have control over his situation. There's no easy answer to give for this contradiction; according to most religions it requires omnipresence and omniscient qualities. Beside the question whether we will be able to get any answers, this contradiction has been a central matter since our earliest understanding of our world. There's a continuous struggle between the turbulence of nature and the position of man in this nature, which man as a conscious being finds hard to accept. Fromm describes this as follows:

> All passions and strivings of man are attempts to find an answer to his existence or, as we may also say, they are an attempt to avoid insanity. (It may be said in passing that the real problem of mental life is not why some people become insane, but rather why most avoid insanity.) Both the mentally healthy and the neurotic are driven by the need to find an answer, the only difference being that one answer corresponds more to the total needs of man, and hence is more conducive to the unfolding of his powers and to his happiness than the other.[9]

Finding an answer to this contradiction is also key to The One Self, which in itself consist of two antagonists, power and fear, to which Zilboorg states:

> Such constant expenditure of psychological energy on the business of preserving life would be impossible if the fear of death were not as constant. The very term "self-preservation" implies an effort against some force of disintegration; the affective aspect of this is fear, fear of death.[10]

This fear of death is just as constant as the need we feel to defend The One Self. But we can't constantly think about it in our daily lives, as we wouldn't be capable of getting anything done, and the constant threat would drive us completely mad. The only way to cope with it, is to suppress this threat, as Zilboorg continues:

> If this fear were as constantly conscious, we should be unable to function normally. It must be properly repressed to keep us living with any modicum of comfort. We know very well that to repress means more than to put away and to forget that which was put away and the place where we put it. It means also to maintain a constant psychological effort to keep the lid on and inwardly never relax our watchfulness.[11]

Individuals who keep denying the actual circumstance they are in and subsequently suppress this real situation and substitute it for something else, can be called neurotic individuals. These are not the few who are singled out and put away in a closed institution. No, this is about all of us. All of us possess, to some degree, the urge to suppress the actual situations in which we find ourselves, and try to imagine our situation in the world as being different. Fromm explains that the 'normal' person has the same characteristics as the common image of a neurotic person in a psychiatric institution:

> The phenomena which we observe in the neurotic person are in principle not different from those we find in the normal. They are only more accentuated, clear-cut, and frequently more accessible to the awareness of the neurotic person than they are in the normal who is not aware of any problem which warrants study.[12]

The suppression by the neurotic person becomes apparent as soon as the mechanism shows temporary signs of malfunctioning. It's the response we all have to the moment of clarity we experience during that romantic walk along the beach with our partner, at the beginning of chapter 1. At that moment it becomes clear to us that we are just a part of nature, and that we've unconsciously known that all along, as Marcuse argues: 'The brute fact of death denies once and for all the reality of a non-repressive existence.'[13] In part one we already made a division into different behavioural types with which The One Self can present itself. We made a distinction between three separate types: the negative type, that tends to have negative thoughts or feelings and has a certain resentment towards the world; the positive type, that takes action and quickly feels at home in every social context; the open type, that views a situation from a distance and experiences a deeper consciousness of, or has deeper insight into, the surrounding world.

When we look at individuals as neurotics, we can take a different view of this tripartition. This division runs parallel to that of part one, but with some differentiation.

3.1 Type 1

A very important characteristic of the neurotic type 1 is that this type retires into his shell, and doesn't dare to look at the outside world, his immediate surroundings, directly in the eye, because this 'big bad world' appears to him as dangerous or unreliable. Taking part in social events isn't high on type 1's agenda, he rather stays home, secure in his own environment. As the type 1 neurotic tries so much to avoid and deny the outside world, he will be more inclined to turn in upon himself. As an important result he will never fully come to bloom as a human being, he will never completely develop himself, or as Becker writes:

> The individual has to protect himself against the world, and he can do this only as any other animal would: by narrowing down the world, shutting off experience, developing an obliviousness both to the terrors of the world and to his own anxieties.[14]

We may also refer to this type as the depressed or introspective neurotic. This neurotic type is very much a hermit of his own feelings. Of course this is not a black-and-white situation. The thoughts of the neurotic type 1 are tinted in various shades of grey. But, when the type 1 neurotic goes to the extreme in his denial of the world, the individual will see only one way out, and that is suicide. In doing so the most important aspect of life is extinguished, which is The One Self, our inner core as we saw in part one. There are different reasons why an individual displays type 1 behaviour at a certain time, for instance: a melancholy world view, a chronic physical disability, feelings of low self-worth or persisting misunderstanding by fellow men about his situation.

Type 1 neurotics are focussed on individual behaviour.

3.2 Type 2

The type 2 neurotic can be characterised as the man in the street. In an industrialised society this means for example that he goes to work every day, lives in a terraced house, has a car parked in front of the door, probably has two children, likes good food, goes on vacation preferably several times a year, and has a host of friends and acquaintances. This 'average' citizen talks about the daily futilities that keep pace with the newspaper headlines of the moment. The world simply is the world to him. He has a hobby which he can wholly plunge himself into. But, beside his own realm of life, he doesn't contemplate much on anything else.

> Most men spare themselves this trouble by keeping their minds on the
> small problems of their lives just as their society maps these problems
> out for them. These are what Kierkegaard called the "immediate" men
> and the "Philistines." They "tranquilize themselves with the trivial"-
> and so they can lead normal lives.[15]

The neurotic type 2 lives here and now. He doesn't go searching, or even want an explanation, for the course of certain events that take place on the global scene. Above all, he is a materialist: his body is his temple, his car is his soul and his house is his kingdom. This average citizen is the example of the modern, industrialised, hedonistic individual.

The type 2 neurotic also is a real consumer. He is never satisfied with what he already owns. Worse still, he craves for what he doesn't own, which automatically results in the next purchase of the newest trending product. The contentment about the newly bought item, however rapidly decreases, also because type 2 is very impressionable to the requirements, values and principles of his peer group, signalling that he should buy the newest trending products.[16] Since the neurotic type 2 matches his choices to the behaviour of his peer group, one can say that he doesn't have much control over himself in the sense of having true free will or an own identity.

Type 2 neurotics are at their best within a group of people.

3.3 Type 3

The type 3 neurotic, just as the type 1 neurotic, is dissatisfied about the material, and according to him, limiting world. He would like to rid himself of it, or at least explore its boundaries. Where type 1's attitude leads to renouncing the worldly issues, type 3 actually explores the world, or creates one for himself. The world needs to be shaped, studied and its possibilities should be used to the full by exploring its limits. Good examples of this type are artists: they create a world of their own, in which they have complete control, for instance by creating a painting or a sculpture. To create, we need to analyse what we want to create. Consciousness of, and reflection on the environment and ourselves are important requirements. After the analysis we've come to reinterpret our own situation or the environment, and we've collected the input necessary to transfer an idea, standpoint, or feeling into an artwork. As such, the type 3 neurotic imposes his own system onto the existing world.

A different example is someone who creates an ideology, which gains followers, mostly represented by type 2 neurotics. The followers in this example are very obedient and present themselves as a group. The leader is the creative individual, the keeper of the idea, who paves the way. And in the negative instance, leading to a totalitarian regime, he knows how to exploit the obedience of his followers well.

Type 3 neurotics are focussed on individual behaviour.

In this chapter we've taken another look at the typification of the behaviour of The One Self from part one. By denying reality, all these neurotic types try to manoeuvre themselves into a well controlled environment and maintain themselves in it. However, it applies for all three types that they are forever inextricably bound by the real, physical, world, and subject to the natural laws of physics. They will eventually die, whether they deny the world, embrace it, or try to recreate it for themselves. This is the tough reality all individuals are faced with, and which leads to the question whether life can be valuable or necessary at all. In the next chapter, we will see that attention, acknowledgement and appreciation for the individual are important aspects for our motivation to think and act.

4 Acknowledgement and Value

The neurotic typification set aside, we all need some kind of acknowledge-ment of our surroundings, ourselves or any other person, even if it were to confirm our behaviour. We prefer to avoid situations or thoughts which can lead to humiliation or shame, especially when they become public. In our actions we rather tend to seek the respect of others, so that we can have a sense of pride and honour about ourselves. Through our actions or thoughts we wish to leave a mark to increase our sense of self-worth. Every individual seeks this kind of acknowledgement in personal engagements -a loving gesture, being there for others-, in physical engagements -sexual needs, an extraordinary sports accomplishment-, spiritual engagements -being an inspiration for others, appreciation for something we came up with, a clear statement, membership of a religious community-, societal engagements -being successful at our job, doing voluntary work-, etc. In the end, we are beings with senses and emotions. We are committed to those we care about, and to what we do in our daily lives.

> But man is not just a blind glob of idling protoplasm, but a creature with a name who lives in a world of symbols and dreams and not merely matter. His sense of self-worth is constituted symbolically, his cherished narcissism feeds on symbols, on an abstract idea of his own worth, an idea composed of sounds, words, and images, in the air, in the mind, on paper. And this means that man's natural yearning for organismic activity, the pleasures of incorporation and expansion, can be fed limitlessly in the domain of symbols and so into immortality.[17]

How we attain this acknowledgement depends on what type of neurotic we are. A compliment given by a type 2 person to a type 1 person, who looks up to the type 2, is extremely valuable to the type 1. For those showing type 2 behaviour, a comment by a type 2 colleague on their stunning new trendy car is the confirmation they've been hoping for. And, for a type 3 person an award from his colleagues, or a special exhibition of his own work, feels like a pat on the back.

To every neurotic type applies, that they like receiving acknowledgement for the effort they put into their activities, in order to escape reality for a moment and be able to feel like a hero.

As discussed before in part two The Individual, everyone seeks personal acknowledgement. We all want to leave a mark, experience a moment of fame, make our contribution to mankind. How little or insignificant these contributions may be, we want to use our capabilities to get the best out of ourselves. Through the acknowledgement we receive, we feel that our sense of self-worth increases.

The appreciation for us, as unique individuals, already begins the moment we are born. The prenatal circumstances in which life is formed, who our parents are, the genetic code we carry with us, all these things establish our uniqueness, even before we enter into this world. During this life we weigh everything that happens to us to its worth: that birthday that's coming up, finally taking a trip to that specific metropolis or visiting that beautiful nature resort; these will become beautiful memories in hindsight. But, the route we take to work every day is a mere routine which is just a good opportunity to take a minute to think about other things. When something occurs less it becomes more unique. We are inclined to value it more. The qualitative aspect of these precious moments is the value we attach to the specific situation or experience. These once-in-a-life-time moments we must treasure, remember well, and preferably document, one way or another. Our daily rituals are trivial, we've done them thousands of times. So we won't remember them specifically. The value we attach to our surroundings, regardless of the neurotic type, is very important. Without value, and this *is* an open door, nothing precious remains. And, what's more precious than a reward?

5 The Reward

What are our needs or longings in this life? Or more personally put: what pushes us to strive for something or someone, by which we gain specific value or some sort of reward? There clearly isn't just one answer to this. The answer to this personal question depends on which neurotic type you ask the question.

The type 1 individuals, especially those who are at the extreme end of this neurotic type, keep denying life and try avoiding every confrontation with reality. For them death comes as a deliverance. The moderate type 1 neurotics are motivated to metaphorically cross that bridge to type 2. Although, when suffering hardship, they are in danger of easily slipping and falling back into their former type 1 behaviour.

A type 2 neurotic wouldn't be that concerned about rewards, more likely, he'd immediately provide for them himself. When he looks around him, he sees his possessions, his career or other accomplishments as his immediate reward. The type 2 strives to acquire as much material possessions he can to show off to his peer neurotics in order to get the affirmation from the group he belongs to. A type 2 neurotic might believe in 'something' after death, but during life he won't be very actively engaged in this by further study.

A type 3 neurotic needs to create something. His reward lies in the acknowledgement he receives for it. This may be a special exhibition of his work, or the many favourable responses of visitors to his website. The acknowledgement by a colleague type 3 neurotic is very important here, even though the artist could be very tempted to accept the bid when a type 2 neurotic is willing to pay an excessive amount of money for one of his works of art. Whether a type 1, 2 or 3 neurotic, the self-conscious emotional being we humans are must eventually always step over that last threshold of life, a step even heroes can't escape from, beyond which awaits actual death. For the type 2 neurotic, this last step may be most confronting, as this neurotic type is the one standing firm, and is in no need of a depressed or creative 'answer' to deny the existing world or to create one of his own. On his deathbed, the neurotic type 2, so attached to possessions, family and friends, will see all that he's built up over the years disappear. Where type 1 and 3 neurotics are confronted with death during life and have attuned to certain behaviour, for type 2 neurotics the confrontation with death, that which he has been trying to avoid all his life, comes at the very end.

Actually, we all leave this earth along the path the type 1 neurotic took, as he finds himself nearest to this -strictly biologically speaking- natural process. Just before our death, when we become aware of the nearing end, the truth of the human insignificance and meaninglessness shows itself most strongly and clearly. The triviality of the appearances we keep up in our daily activities becomes evident at such a moment. At the time of our death, our life appears clearest in our minds. There is no more opportunity for denial, for seeking an excuse to hide behind. The denial of reality, felt by type 1 neurotics as something they can't cope with, is felt by everyone of us on our deathbeds. The control over the situation is completely lost, the fear of death, the disappearance of The One Self, has taken over completely, and we can no longer avoid it.

When there is no reward left in this world, for any of the three neurotic types, nothing to which they can cling to, with no assurance that they themselves, their ideas or actions will live on, then it becomes clear that this world is a distant cold spot to live in. The biological process that takes place, death, the natural end of our existence, is a hard, but unavoidable reality. To give it a sense of purpose, the individual must find it in his own subjective truth. Exemplary of this are the various existing philosophies of life. Many of them provide the promise of an eternal resting place. They provide comfort in the shape of a merciful supreme being, and sketch the most idyllic spot for The One Self to continue throughout eternity.

6 Cross Connections

In this chapter we will once more make cross connections between the previous chapters. For each of the three neurotic types we will look at what influences them, regarding consciousness, the heroic role, feelings of acknowledgement and value, and the intended reward. This time too, we will avoid the processual, objective description of the previous chapters and provide a more common, practical infill of the developments. The descriptions and examples are of course meant to clarify the process and don't provide an absolute reflection of situations in daily life.

6.1 Consciousness

The world around us, the objective reality, is omnipresent, even when we ourselves are long gone. This objective reality presents itself to us as an accomplished fact. The tree in the park will always be the same tree. Whether in spring or fall, this tree will maintain the same characteristics. If we can't depend on reality, or reality changes constantly, we loose our foothold in our surroundings, loose our grip on our actions, and we will probably go mad. But we colour the objective reality: when we fall in love, the same tree in the park becomes a beautiful tree under which we like to repose with our loved one. Yet, when we're depressed this tree becomes a grey obstacle on our shortest route through the park. By colouring the objective reality, we create our own subjective truth. So, as humans, we recognise subjectivity. Nature, our living environment, only knows objectivity. Nature simply follows the path of cause and effect with no regard for the consequences. It is a process that simply happens, a process where reality isn't coloured in in any way, or as Robert Green Ingersoll expressed it: There are in nature neither rewards nor punishments - there are consequences.[18]

Above all, we need truth to find our way in this world, and to be able to communicate about one and the same environment. Savater points this out:

> The [...] pitfall here is the opinion that the concept of 'truth' doesn't necessarily always need to have a direct, and stable relationship with reality. Of course, truth isn't stable, far from it. But, truth as a temporary, pliable outcome of public and clear arguments, understood by all, is of utmost importance. The capacity of the human race to survive is clearly inseparably bond to a fundamental form of 'truth' as the outcome of our perceptions of all independent existence.[19]

At important moments in our lives the natural objective reality and our human subjective truth can collide. For instance, it feels as an utter injustice when one of our loved ones passes away. We expect nature to adjust itself, because we care so dearly about this person, but of course it doesn't. Nature knows no right or wrong, no sympathy or antipathy. In this case the outcome of the biological process, the death of a loved one, doesn't change by the presence of a subjective person. During that perfect walk along the beach with our love, this inevitable reality can surprise us at any moment, and tear us loose from the truth we've compiled for ourselves.

> He is part of nature, subject to her physical laws and unable to change them, yet he transcends the rest of nature. He is set apart while being a part; he is homeless, yet chained to the home he shares with all creatures. Cast into this world at an accidental place and time, he is forced out of it, again accidentally. Being aware of himself, he realizes his powerlessness and the limitations of his existence. He visualizes his own end: death. Never is he free from the dichotomy of his existence: he cannot rid himself of his mind, even if he should want to; he cannot rid himself of his body as long as he is alive – and his body makes him want to be alive.[20]

We can, of course, influence the objective world by 'taking nature into our own hands', for example, by making a house out of natural materials, or by drilling for oil and processing it to make all kinds of products. The purpose of this is that the objective world, as opposed to us, doesn't have consciousness and doesn't need to accommodate to our demands or desires. Just because we can give meaning to things around us, doesn't mean that these things have meaning of their own. For instance, no other being than the human can see figures such as a sheep in the shapes of the clouds. But of course we're not certain if the average sheep could imagine a congener in the shape of the clouds, probably more likely a large green meadow with juicy grass to graze. Humans, on the other hand, have an innate 'antenna' to recognise shapes and interpret them as something tangible.

> The reason for this is that the human mind always looks for regularity and order, even when they aren't there. This applies to very basis perceptual processes, such as seeing the shape of a man in the moon, or a face in the clouds. Nature draws up an arbitrary pattern of blotches, and we see something in them, mostly faces, creepy men or other biological forms.[21]

As a subjective being, man is dependent on the possibilities and inhibitions of his own body. In the social context, there are different factors that determine how we behave in our lives. These can be roughly divided into internal and external factors.

Internal factors are, for instance, the information stored in our genes, the chemical household of our body (whether we produce the right substances such as hormones, white blood cells etc.), and which and how many connections are made between the neurons in our brains. Every person is unique the moment he or she is born. But the make-up of our brains and the genetic material already determine largely how our bodies will function.[22] There are many influential factors from the moment the foetus starts developing in the uterus, such as the amount and diversity of the nourishment that is fed via the placenta, the use of alcohol, tobacco and medicine by the mother during pregnancy. This affects for example, the measure of our aggressive behaviour,[23] or our chances of contracting certain disorders and personality traits, such as liability for substance abuses like alcoholism (55% genetically determined), schizophrenia (80%), and also intelligence (88%).[24] Of course, this doesn't mean that if a person has a tendency to alcoholism, this person would 'automatically' become an alcoholic. Beside a genetic tendency, we must also include social factors, upbringing etc., which can have a decisive impact, for example, by training our brains. The neurons in our brains send information to each other via many connections between the synapses, or nerve endings. By repetitively activating the same neuron, a nervous connection -a fixed pattern with strong synapses- is formed, which sends information easier or faster than other nervous connections with a more flexible pattern.[25] By repeatedly establishing the same behaviour, we activate the same neurons, and by practising hard we can thus learn something new. From our own experience we know that learning how to swim isn't very easy in the beginning. During those first lessons we're busy with various things at the same time, our body needs to process all kinds of new information simultaneously: our arms and legs need to make controlled movements, we must learn to keep ourselves afloat in the water, we must keep sight of our environment, and, most of all, we must make sure we don't drawn. By practising a lot this programme of movements is locked into our brains, and, years later we won't need to consciously think about it whenever we jump into the pool. In the same way we can look at a young violinist of only 5 years old. By completely committing to the techniques to learning how to play the violin, this boy's brains have been trained to be able to give a concert at such a young age.[26]

> The more often the neurons are stimulated, the more securely a lasting connection is established. The more often we punch in a telephone number, the better we remember it. Learning emotional responses works the same way. Once connections are made, repetition keeps them alive.[27]

Beside the internal factors, there are the external factors, such as the social environment in which we grow up (whether living in a slum or in a villa), the role of our parents (whether they give us a strict upbringing or provide us with all the freedom we want, or whether we learn to say thank you or just take anything we like without asking), engaging into making social contacts or keeping them at bay. These factors combined largely determine how our body reacts to stimuli under certain circumstances. Even so, we can of course still intervene. The five year old, who can already play fantastic violin, can at any moment decide he'd rather go out to play, because engaging in social contacts is stimulated by the parents, or simply because playing with other kids is more fun at that moment.

On top of these internal and external factors, which combined lead to certain behaviour, the insight, self-knowledge, and self-control are the greatest individual challenges. When a person is too dependent on internal and external behavioural factors, this person will behave accordingly. When the chemical substances in the body are out of balance, a person could tend to show feelings of depression. When we have the right muscular length or mass and a large lung capacity, it will be easier for us to excel at sports than without these beneficial characteristics. Self-knowledge can play an important role here to analyse the behaviour that is formed by the internal and external factors. This knowledge can then be used to gain insight into future situations, to evaluate them better and thus correct our own behaviour. Composure subsequently leads us to excel in sports, to climb the highest mountaintops, and to create the finest works of art. Self-knowledge, insight and self-control are our greatest merits, which separate us from everything else in this world, which really make us human. The best thing is to develop The One Self in such a way, that it becomes an individual master piece. And this is a goal that reaches further than our objective environment and our subjective characteristics, our internal and external behavioural factors combined.

6.2 Hero

When reviewing chapter 1 of part two, the social development, we see an interesting parallel with the role the hero fulfils. In phase 1 of the social development, i.e. the natural system, the divine is the highest goal. After his heroic deed, and after his death, the hero can be saved and live on in the afterlife. When the development of the social society reaches its second phase, the divine loses its central position in society. Of course, this doesn't mean that people have less need of spirituality, the quest for the meaning of life generally remains. As to heroism, a shift takes place from the heavenly divine to the earthly mortal. Our loved one becomes the hero, the one we adore, and who gives meaning to our life. Living happily together is now the highest goal. This new focus of the individual on the partner in life is described by Becker:

> He fixed his urge to cosmic heroism onto *another person* in the form
> of a love object. The self-glorification that he needed in his innermost
> nature he now looked for in the love partner. The love partner becomes
> the divine ideal within which to fulfill one's life. All spiritual and moral
> needs now become focussed in one individual. Spirituality, which once
> referred to another dimension of things, is now brought down to this
> earth and given form in another individual human being.[28]

By the development from phase 2 to phase 3, that of communication, the partnership in turn loses its central role. We find that our partner cannot fulfil the role of the saviour we project on them. We see that he or she, just as we ourselves, is a finite creature with human -thus limited- possibilities, while the high demands, that we place on our partner, continue to exist.

> When we look for the "perfect" human object we are looking for
> someone who allows us to express our will completely, without any
> frustration or false notes. We want an object that reflects a truly ideal
> image of ourselves.[29]

Unfortunately, a future partner can never live up to our requirements. This ideal image simply can't be achieved. Consequently, the inescapable imperfection affects us too. We are increasingly busy with our own personality, we strive for more personal perfection, we become again, and ever more, dependent on ourselves. In this third phase of the social development we ourselves become the hero, and we strive to gain acknowledgement and appreciation from our fellow men for who we are and what we do. During this process, our extrovert expressions change into internal experiences, where each of us strives for self-realisation. Only when we fully accept our true selves, will we develop as individuals, and only then will we be free of our submissive stance towards others, and other forms of dependence. As the Greek poet Pindar expressed (and which has become especially noted through Nietzsche's citation): 'You should become what you are.'[30] Fromm describes this:

> Every act of submissive worship is an act of alienation and idolatry in
> this sense. What is frequently called "love" is often nothing but this
> idolatrous phenomenon of alienation; only that not God or an idol, but
> another person is worshiped in this way. The "loving" person in this
> type of submissive relationship, projects all his or her love, strength,
> thought, into the other person, and experiences the loved person as a
> superior being, finding satisfaction in complete submission and wor-
> ship. This does not only mean that he fails to experience the loved
> person as a human being in his or her reality, but that he does not
> experience *himself* in his full reality, as the bearer of productive human
> powers. Just as in the case of religious idolatry, he has projected all his
> richness into the other person, and experiences this richness not any
> more as something which is his, but as something alien from himself,
> deposited in somebody else, with which he can get in touch only by
> submission to, or submergence in the other person.[31]

So, during this process, our perspective changes. In phase 1 we, as individuals, look up to the divine hero, in phase 2 we look to our side, to our earthly love partner, and in phase 3 we look inward and find the hero in ourselves by following through the process to complete self-realisation. In this last phase, all the requirements are present for complete inner contemplation, for self-development, which enables us to become heroes. The difficulty of this third phase is that the self-fabricated or self-enforced system has no legitimacy. In the external projection of the hero in phase 1 or 2, there is a structure or a system, in which the individual dedication is controlled. In these phases there is a religious community, which ensures that 'all noses point in the same direction'. And in matrimony there are written and un-written agreements on living together. But, who controls the self-realisation in phase 3? What are the rules? What is right, and what is wrong? During this process, can you be critical enough about yourself? Any feedback from a group is hardly likely, as this is a highly individual process. A group wise exchange of ideas or experiences is very difficult. We are our own judges, which is why insight, self-knowledge, and self-control are of the utmost importance in this phase.

Following this line of thought there are no more phases left after phase 3. Our perspective won't change again. Most important now is to maintain the current situation for as long as possible, to prevent us from gliding back into a former phase. In reviewing this process, we see that the hero changes from an anonymous individual, who lives in a group in phase 1, who stands close to nature and is oppressed by a dictator, to an individual in a technocracy in phase 3, who strives for the completion of self-realisation, and shares his experiences with everyone around the world, hoping for recognition.

6.3 The Neurotic Types

There is a certain pattern of expectations, roughly outlined of course, of the behaviour the neurotic has of himself, just as his surroundings have of him. Following are two examples where the effects between different groups of neurotic types, as well as those within one group of the same neurotic type are discussed.

The first example shows the differences in the setup of a television show, when adjusting for the target groups of neurotic types 2 and 3.
A television quiz is targeted at neurotic type 2 individuals. A type 2 neurotic is sensitive to all things material, so there's a large sum of money to win in a show with much spectacle. To win the main prize, however, there mustn't be too high an obstacle to overcome. Above all, it must be entertaining,

even for the type 2 viewer. The contestant can win by answering a number of simple questions. Or, even more to the point, the candidate no longer needs to answer questions at all, he only needs to open a numbered box. The tension of excitement is raised by the quiz master, who postpones the moment of truth for as long as possible, supported by dramatic music.

A quiz targeting the type 3 neurotic is quite the opposite. The studio is quiet, almost soberly decorated, and there's no roaring audience. The contestants are tested on their knowledge, whereby the quiz, which is rich in content, is much more complicated than the quiz for the type 2 neurotic. And the financial reward, by comparison, is often far smaller, and sometimes merely exists of the acknowledgement of having won.

The stage decoration, the intro tune, the rhythm of the broadcast, the quiz master, all are tuned to the corresponding group.

The second example reveals the horizontal stratification of a society in the second phase of the social development.

Street youths take up a position somewhere at the bottom of the social ladder. They are often seen as such by the rest of society. However, just like everyone else, these youths want personal acknowledgement instead of just being in a world where all has been thought out and decided for them. Every individual wants to make his own contribution, and wants to see the effects of his actions reflected in the world. This gives him a sense of involvement and appreciation. Street youths want their own spot in society. To get them more involved, or in any case, get rid of the trouble they cause, the municipality provides resources for these youths to choose, build, and decorate their own hangout. By creating their own environment, these youths gain a certain rightful place within society.

Thus, they climb up a rung on the social ladder. But if this hangout is vandalised by another group of youths, the youths who built the hangout will call that a-social behaviour. So, they now blame a group, standing slightly lower on the social ladder, for something they were previously blamed for by the rest of society.

It applies to all neurotic types, that they respond to or look upon the behaviour of the other two neurotic types differently. The expectations, demands, satisfactions or rewards for each type differ per situation. Apart from these two examples, we can make more specific comparisons between these three types.

How does the neurotic type 1 look upon the other two types?
A type 1 neurotic especially looks up to type 2 neurotics. From the type 1's point of view, the type 2 neurotics know exactly how things work in this world, they know the right people, they are shrewd and understand the etiquette of the modern, worldly life because they happily embrace it. A type 1 neurotic rather has difficulty to feel at home in such a world and wonders how he should present himself. Thus he is awe stricken by the type 2 neurotics, and he will show himself serviceable to them. In extreme cases the type 1 neurotic may show to be very dependent on type 2 neurotics, as they need type 2 neurotics to keep in touch with the outside world.
A type 1 neurotic sometimes also looks up to type 3 neurotics. The creative, designing aspect of type 3 is especially appealing to him. The type 3 neurotic is also very focussed on individual behaviour. He creates a world of his own, something the type 1 neurotic is familiar with as well, but this type translates it negatively. A type 1 neurotic, who has tendencies to type 3 behaviour, will in that respect disapprove of the behaviour of type 2 neurotics, because they are too focussed on earthly matters, on the present, and not on the safe haven that the self-created world provides for him.

How does the neurotic type 2 look upon the other two types?
The type 2 neurotic is foremost a team player, a social person who observes other type 2 neurotics, and matches his behaviour to theirs. This is how the individual strengthens the bonds he has within the group, and the cohesion within the group remains consistent. Group cohesion, in part, is also a way to camouflage fear, as it ensures that outsiders are easily recognised. Thus they cannot easily take part in the group, unless of course they comply with the demands of the group. In this way, the group largely determines the identity of the individual within the group.
How strong a bond can be within a group can be seen in a study by Solomon Asch on the so-called 'bystander effect'. It appears that individuals behave according to the values determined by the group, they conform to these values in order not to fall out of tune with the rest of the group. Goldacre describes this experiment:

> It's easy to forget the phenomenal impact of conformity. You doubt-
> less think of yourself as a fairly independent-minded person, and you
> know what you think. I would suggest that the same beliefs were held
> by the subjects of Solomon Asch's experiments into social conform-
> ity. These subjects were placed near one end of a line of actors who

presented themselves as fellow experimental subjects but were actually in cahoots with the experimenters. Cards were held up with one line marked on each of them, and then another card was held up with three lines of different lengths: six inches, eight inches, ten inches. Everyone called out in turn which line on the second card was the same length as the line on the first. For six of the eighteen pairs of cards the accomplices gave the correct answer, but for the other twelve they called out the wrong answer. In all but a quarter of the cases, the experimental subjects went along with the incorrect answer from the crowd of accomplices on one or more occasions, defying the clear evidence of their own senses.[32]

This example shows all the more the remarkable effect conformity has on our behaviour because the group has a mere temporary nature. As the guinea pigs in this experiment, we don't know the other people standing in line. The study takes place in a lab, not even in the real world. We know that we'll soon be standing outside again. The results of the study don't affect us, in the sense that there's no gain or loss in it for us. This changes when such things happen in real life where there's a definite loss or gain. There are known cases where a person cries for help while drowning. Passers-by stand along side, watching the event, and none take action to save this person. Or, another case where someone's lying in the middle of a busy street in a large city, moaning with pain and evidently in need of help, but everyone just walks by.[33] No one makes a move, because the cohesion within the group of passers-by would then be compromised, and as individuals we would have to step out of the group act to give assistance. It's much safer to conform to group behaviour, and so do nothing, like all the rest. These instances show that the influence of a group on individual behaviour can be tremendous, and can have harmful, even fatal consequences, for someone who doesn't belong to this group.

Another important motivation for mirroring each other's behaviour as members of a group is the so-called mimetic desire, also known as the effect of keeping up with the Joneses, meaning what the neighbour possesses the type 2 neurotic also wants to posses. This mimetic desire has the effect that the type 2 neurotic purchases things just 'for the sake of having them', not because they're functionally necessary, or because they'll be in use long after the purchase. This temporary desire for possessions is but a fancy. However, it acknowledges and strengthens the sentiment that the type 2 neurotic is part of a group. In turn, this strengthens the urge to mirror each others behaviour, until everyone wears the same outfit or possesses the very car the group dictates, thereby coming full circle.

The behaviour the group members show among themselves thus focusses on conformity. The motivation behind this desire is envy. The neighbour possesses more, and to level out the difference we need to join in. So, we buy the wardrobe and we book that vacation to match the behaviour of the group in order to secure our own status in it. Thus, owning up to the demands of the group becomes a measure for the individual status. This status must be maintained constantly. The danger that awaits us is the fear of loosing status, loosing our image, because then we no longer live up to the expectations of the group. A situation can then arise where we lose the bond with the group. This is a serious threat, especially for a type 2 neurotic, being a group person. Then we'll be on our own, we'll become individual, and there's a great chance that we shift into becoming a type 1 or type 3 neurotic. The fear of loosing status is explained by Botton:

> A worry, so pernicious as to be capable of ruining extended stretches
> of our lives, that we are in danger of failing to conform to the ideals of
> success laid down by our society and that we may as a result be stripped
> of dignity and respect; a worry that we are currently occupying too
> modest a rung or are about to fall to a lower one.[34]

For the type 2 neurotic this especially means fighting for maintaining a standard of material possessions. An 'addiction' to the so-called hedonic treadmill[35] lies in waiting. To live up to every latest fashion statement, the newest products must be bought. Even though we get used to this, we nevertheless keep running along in the same treadmill, and new purchases follow. The effects of the hedonic treadmill, the mimetic desire and status anxiety, keep us motivated for a new purchase, as Wilkinson and Pickett summarise:

> Too often consumerism is regarded as if it reflected a fundamental
> human material self-interest and possessiveness. That, however, could
> hardly be further from the truth. Our almost neurotic need to shop
> and consume is instead a reflection of how deeply social we are. Living
> in unequal and individualistic societies, we use possessions to show
> ourselves in a good light, to make a positive impression, and to avoid
> appearing incompetent or inadequate in the eyes of others. Consumer-
> ism shows how powerfully we are affected by each other.[36]

If the purchase of goods would boost our egos, or bring us one step closer to the wealth we set our minds on, then the background processes simply function as cogs in automised machinery on the way to ultimate bliss. It turns out, however, that from a certain moment the accumulation of possessions has no more effect on our well-being; we no longer gain happiness through it.[37] Again Wilkinson en Pickett:

> If an important part of consumerism is driven by emulation, status competition, or simply having to run to keep up with everyone else, and is basically about social appearances and position, this would explain why we continue to pursue economic growth despite its apparent lack of benefits. [...] Once we have enough of the necessities of life, it is the relativities which matter.[38]

Buying new things becomes an automatic response to certain stimuli. It's not about the purchase of the product itself or the value it represents. It's rather about the act of purchasing, and the novelty of the product fades as soon as it is unpacked.

> [There is a]... tendency for shopping pleasure to become detached from the reality and utility of the goods. Shopping is no longer so much about the gratification of desire as the thrill of desire itself, which must be constantly renewed. The actual purchases become less and less satisfying. Potential is always infinite but whatever is chosen is always finite. For the addict of potential every climax is an anticlimax. The magical talisman is revealed as mundane and the transcendent shopper returns to the familiar, disappointing self. Frequently the gorgeous clothes are never worn, the amazing gadget never used, the fascinating book never read and the thrilling CD never played.[39]

Before we decide which purchases to make, we let ourselves be influenced by our environment. Obviously, friends and family are very important at a personal level. At a more impersonal, though still rather influential, level are the commercial companies. By making commercials they also use the effect of mimetic desire. A company advertises a product, showing the people are happy and are liked by everyone else. So when we buy this product, we are made to believe that this will happen to us as well, and that our friends will also think we're terrific. And we will be encouraged to share this product via the internet, so that other friends will be poked to buy that product. At least, that's what the commercial company hopes for.

Type 2 neurotics are moderately interested in type 3 neurotics, who, in their view, are too erudite and, as far as for example conversation topics are concerned, stand too far apart from them. Type 2 neurotics are only interested in type 1 neurotics when they are family. From the type 1 neurotic's standpoint, a type 2 neurotic is too positive-minded, has too much of a central position in life to become somber or to turn his back on the world.

How does the type 3 neurotic look upon the other two types?

A type 3 neurotic actually looks at all the neurotic types. He needs all the input from his environment to be the maker of a valuable creation. The creative process, however, regularly contains a dismissive element, through the aversion of the 'negative' world housed by the type 1 neurotic, and the disgust of the world of the type 2 neurotic, which he abhors for its bourgeois and conformist character. A type 3 neurotic looks at both of the other neurotic types, but also at himself. For, he is the greatest critic of his creative processes. During his life the type 3 neurotic gains acknowledgement for his creations from other type 3 neurotics, as intellectuals among themselves. The acknowledgement from the community at large, mainly consisting of type 2 neurotics, usually comes after his death, as the meaning and value of his artwork must first sink in. A type 3 neurotic, through his insights, visions and ideas which result in creations, actually strides ahead of the type 2 neurotic. The type 2 only later arrives at the museum, unfamiliar with the artist's creative idea's, and probably defends his own presence by saying 'he was such a well-known artist'. From the type 3 neurotic's standpoint, the type 2 neurotic is a bourgeois, somewhat naive person who isn't really interested in the world. Type 3 neurotics don't understand that type 2 neurotics can be so easily content with, or so disinterested in, the world as it presents itself.

> The key to the creative type is that he is separated out of the common pool of shared meanings. There is something in his life experience that makes him take in the world as a *problem*; as a result he has to make personal sense out of it. This holds true for all creative people to a greater or lesser extent, but it is especially obvious with the artist. Existence becomes a problem that needs an ideal answer; but when you no longer accept the collective solution to the problem of existence, then you must fashion your own. The work of art is, then, the ideal answer of the creative type to the problem of existence as he takes it

> in-not only the existence of the external world, but especially his own:
> who he is as a painfully separate person with nothing shared to lean
> on. He has to answer to the burden of his extreme individuation, his
> so painful isolation.[40]

This tripartition of neurotic types can be explained in various ways. The neurotic types 1 and 3 feel greater urgency to show responsibility for their behaviour than the neurotic type 2. These two types are more easily recognised as individuals as opposed to the type 2 neurotics, who prefer not to break with the safety of the group. Traditionally most people belong to the type 2 neurotic, and thus they dictate the standards of society. Deviations from the group are noted and scrutinised.

Another way of looking at the neurotic types is by categorising them into dependent and independent individuals. A type 2 neurotic would then be a dependent individual, because he maintains himself within a group, and as such he is very dependent on what the group expects of him. Type 1 and 3 neurotics are independent. These are individuals who develop their own opinions and/or ideas to give their life meaning. A type 1 neurotic can't come up with an answer that satisfies him, and is ceased by apprehension. The type 3 neurotic, however, possesses the power to overcome this, by giving it an intellectual or artistic turn.

Yet another way of observing these types is by looking at possible genetic differences. Is there scientific proof explaining the origin of the different neurotic type's behaviour? It appears that people with a more active right brain half are more introvert and pessimistic. By that measure people with a more active left brain half are more self-assured, more positive.

> People whose right brain half is more active and who have less con-
> trol over their negative emotions tend to be introverted, pessimistic,
> and often suspicious. They see catastrophe looming in the slightest
> misfortune, have a relatively higher incidence of depression, and in
> general tend to be unhappy. People with a significantly stronger left
> prefrontal cortex, on the other hand, usually prove to be true Sunday's
> children. They are self-confident, optimistic, and often in high spirits.
> They find it easy to be around others and seem to have been born with
> the ability to see life's sunny side.[41]

It's good to keep in mind here, that human behaviour is hardly ever engaged automatically. There are many factors that have a continuing influence on our behaviour, as we've already seen in chapter 1 of part one. And it would be wrong to think that once an individual shows certain behaviour, this individual will always show that specific behaviour. A change in the neurotic type can take place swiftly, or over a number of years. When an individual shows signs of behaviour of another neurotic type, this behaviour in turn may be very brief, or persist for several years with possible intermittent fluctuations to both of the other behavioural types. There will also be very few individuals who completely match the description of type 1, 2 or 3 behaviour. While displaying a certain type of behaviour, there will always be aspects of the other behavioural types present, to a greater or lesser degree, which combined represent the total behaviour of an individual.

Then the questions arise: why is it so difficult to change one's behaviour?, why do people so stubbornly stick to their role in their specific neurotic type? In the first paragraph of chapter 6, we already discussed the presence of internal factors (e.g. information stored in our genes) and external factors (e.g. the social environment) that influence our behaviour. And, in chapter 1 we already saw that human behaviour doesn't change rapidly, because current behaviour is based on past behaviour, thoughts and decisions. For continuity's sake, we need to confirm our present behaviour to justify ourselves. This gives us a safe and secure feeling, because it's familiar ground. In this way, The One Self has control over a situation, and thus won't be threatened. We'd completely lose our way, if these ingrained certainties would actually differ every day. Of course, we vary them slightly (with our choice of food, clothes, travel destinations), but these are variations to a far stricter underlying system.

When we look at the specific neurotic types we see that type 1 looks up to type 2. The type 1 neurotic doesn't have the attitude, energy or possibilities to join the group of type 2. Type 1 is hindered especially because the present behaviour is based on previous behaviour. This type wants to see his own behaviour reaffirmed time and again. If he took that step and joined the group of type 2 it would be a breach with those years he's spent as a type 1, a denial of his own history, the choices he made, his life up to then. The same applies to the neurotic types 2 and 3. They too, are anchored in their typical behaviour. They constantly reaffirm their behaviour, whether on automatic pilot or consciously, in order not to have to switch to a different neurotic type, thereby risking the loss of the securities that have been built up over the years.

In 'Fear of Freedom' Fromm[42] makes the same sort of classification into neurotic types through pseudo thinking, feeling, and wanting by individuals.

This refers to that which we ought to think, feel and want, e.g. by peer pressure, or more generally by the demands of society on its citizens. Contrary to this is individual thinking, feeling and wanting, which is an original pure principle. It may even go so far that the pseudo self will completely take over the original self. In such a situation the individual may still think that he is making his own decisions, but actually he is conforming to what is expected of him by his surroundings. Consequently the actual original desires or fears are completely repressed. The original self is traded in for the pseudo self, and from then on the individual matches his behaviour to the expectations of others. The group determines the identity of the individual, who actually no longer has an own identity, but a pseudo identity. An individual who takes on so many characteristics of a certain type of behaviour, for instance outer appearances or a manner of speaking, actually shows the stereotypical behaviour of the group. One important advantage of the pseudo self is that it provides the individual with the security of the group. He thus maintains control of his life, even though it's just a sham. The repetitive approval of certain behaviour by other members of the group can lead to individuals falling into automatisms, the so-called automatic conformism. This is expressed, for example, in the choice of clothes, political views, and television programmes. We could say that the pseudo self provides the individual with a cover against real life, true authentic thinking, and the authentic emotions that go with it, in just the same way as the neurotic tries to escape reality. The description above applies most to the neurotic type 2 and least to the neurotic types 1 and 3. The neurotic type 1 cannot maintain the authentic individual in this world, and turns in upon himself. The neurotic type 3, however, is capable of maintaining his authentic self, which gives him energy to create his own world, or at least seek it.

So far we have seen that there are various factors to ensure that a neurotic type maintains certain behaviour. However, there definitely are methods to change the neurotic type, even from one moment to the next, in the same way The One Self's control over a situation can suddenly change, from having control (power) to loosing it (fear), and vice versa. An individual showing the behaviour of a type 1 neurotic is medicated against his depression, and afterwards he 'feels' like a type 2 or 3 neurotic. A type 2 neurotic may make a fantastic discovery, temporarily taking steps towards the type 3 neurotic. An author, being a type 3 neurotic, gets a writer's block and shifts to the type 2 or 1 neurotic. These are examples of a temporary switch by the different neurotic types. But, there's more needed for a long lasting, even permanent, switch. In this case, profound decisions are needed which determine a longer period, or even the rest, of our lives. One example is that of a near-death experience after which the individual involved gains a completely different look on life.[43] Before the event, he pursued a career, a beautiful house, a big car, and other material possessions. But, after his return to life, he often doesn't care for these things anymore. Family and friends become more important, and there's a deeper consciousness and experience of the world around him. Often the fear of death disappears, because the individual underwent the near-death experience as something pleasant and profoundly beautiful. Another example is someone, who, by intense dedication or conviction, achieves a permanent change of attitude, such as a monk, who, after years of meditation or prayer in total isolation, gains a deep insight. In both cases the individuals have attuned to the behaviour of the neurotic type 3, or the open type of The One Self from part one. On a more practical level, individuals adjust their behaviour whenever there's a big change in their lives, such as a marriage or move to a very different place.[44] Yet another example is actually using the power of the group. Individuals who have gone down in the world, and lead a life at the bottom end of society, can change their look on life when they change their environment, and join a group with a different set of values and principles. The new group member will then start behaving according to the prevailing group behaviour. Give these individuals a project or task and they'll gain purpose in their lives, give them regularity, give them the protection of the group, let them accept and respect the standards and values of the group, and then their behaviour will change.

But, there are also certain moments in our lives, when we don't need intense meditation or undergo a near-death experience to change into an other neurotic type. The midlife crisis is a well-known confrontation that just about everyone goes through at middle age. This is a point in life, when we possess and have experienced all things we should have according to the group we are part of. With the individual living in an industrialised society in mind, this probably mostly amounts to a relationship, a car, a house, a career and children, and also to having made various grand vacations. In the midlife crisis it becomes clear, that our 'own' decisions, almost never are our own. The motivation most often stems from the group, consciously or unconsciously. In a period of self-reflection it becomes clear that the self-value is under pressure, because it actually appears to be the group value. Subsequently we turn to vital questions of life: what have I actually done with my life so far?; and what can I do that I really want for myself?

6.4 Acknowledgement and Value

Acknowledgement

We attribute value to people, objects, situations, and various other matters that we care about. We may for example have an emotional, social or financial relationship with them. And, the value increases, for instance in matters which we've saved a long time for, in the people we've long expected to meet, or an old dream that finally comes true. We can use this value for personal acknowledgement. In general, by possessing valuable objects we show others our accomplishments that have provided us financial independence, we show others that we've 'made it to the top'. Or, by going on a vacation and taking part in various exiting, extreme activities, we expose ourselves as opportunist daredevils, who 'just go ahead and do' such things. The approving nods or exited responses by family and friends following upon our display are personal affirmations of having made the right choice, they flatter our ego. Through a combination of liberalism and capitalism in phase 2 of the social development, acknowledgements are usually expressed financially in the amount of salary the employee receives for the jobs he's done. At the end of this second phase individual prosperity on the whole has exceeded sufficiency. And the society can amply support the need of various collective services, by which raising employees' wages becomes unnecessary or at least doesn't contribute to an absolute sense of personal happiness. It's more about relative riches or poverty, the measure of prosperity we experience relative to our fellow-man which is emotionally expressed in pride or shame.

> To be observed, to be attended to, to be taken notice of with sympathy, complacency, and approbation, are all the advantages which we can propose to derive from it. It is the *vanity, not the ease or the pleasure,* which interests us. But vanity is always founded upon the belief of our being the object of attention and approbation. The rich man *glories* in his riches, because he feels that they naturally draw upon him the attention of the world, and that mankind are disposed to go along with him in all the agreeable emotions with which the advantages of his situation so readily inspire him.... The poor man, on the contrary, is *ashamed* of his poverty. He feels that it either places him out of sight of mankind, or, that if they take any notice of him, they have, however, scarce any fellow feeling with the misery and distress which he suffers....[45]

The prosperity in the modern industrialised world has increased enormously after the Second World War. After the terrible destructions of this war most of the survivors experienced the same miserable situation. By putting their shoulders to the wheel, they rebuilt their country. This forced situation compelled all to strive for the same goals. Everyone knew the recent history and its abominations, and by contrast, the value and meaning of a better future. Fast-forward to over 60 years, and the industrialised citizen is born in a world in which everything already exists; we are born into a world without having to rebuild the cities, without having to reconstruct our lives to move ahead. This makes it harder for us individually to see our own constructs in this world. We want to build on and, especially during adolescence, we prefer to completely change the present social system. The acknowledgement that we as individuals strive for can also be seen as a form of power, because then we are in the spotlights, we are the momentary heroes. Apart from the economic enrichment in the capitalist system there must also be room for personal acknowledgement:

> While capitalism may be capable of creating enormous amount of wealth, it will continue to fail to satisfy the human desire for equal recognition, or *isothymia*. With the division of labor come differences in the dignity of different occupations: garbage men and busboys will always be treated with less respect than brain surgeons or football stars, while the unemployed will have less dignity yet. In prosperous democracies, the problem of poverty has been transformed from one of natural need, into one of recognition. The real injury that is done to poor or homeless people is less to their physical well-being than to their dignity.[46]

The tension of gaining personal acknowledgement and value is pressured even more in phase 3 of the social development. For, what happens when cars and bread are automatically produced and distributed from the factories, where the assembly robots are working 24 hours a day? The employees are needed less and less. The production process thus largely becomes detached from our own physical or mental contributions. How do we attach value to all that surrounds us within a society, which in this phase almost solely exists to provide services, and where the clear individual goal of producing an end product goes missing? Is this the end of the development of society and humankind? To what end are we driven to take action when everything has already been taken care of? Is this the moment in which we can suffice by sitting in a chair, because all the work is being done for us?

The main attraction for this modern human will then be the internet, as we've concluded in part two in the chapter The Social Development. The internet serves as a huge stage for our acting talents. This is where we can put everything up on display to a worldwide audience. But, if everyone joins in, will it deliver us the individual acknowledgement we desperately need? Will we not become anonymous long dozen personalities, venting ourselves with some special trick in the virtual world?

It remains important for individuals to be able to make their own contribution to a product, something for which they must make an individual effort, and subsequently be able to use it, or to be able to observe it being used and to be able to share with others that they produced it. This provides us with extra motivation and ensures an increase in our self-confidence, which is how we can add value to everything around us.

At the end of phase 3 the personal development gains a central role. In this phase the self-realisation into a real, complete and authentic human being takes place. If the modern society doesn't allow us to make our own imprint on society, a way to gain acknowledgement for ourselves and increase our value for the world, we can sink into apathy. This will then be a world of simple existence without there being a portion, however small, to call *our own*.

Value

In a society at the beginning of phase 2 of the social development there still is a measure of segregation. At any given time every individual belongs to a certain group. The church, the school, the political party, the club, etc. are groups bearing distinct profiles, and they shape social division. A lot of importance is attached to maintaining the group: important factors are the group cohesion and the reflection of group behaviour by the individual members of the group. If, as an individual member, you transgress group etiquette, you will feel ashamed of your deviant behaviour.

In the course of phase 2 of the social development this segregation, as we've seen before in the process of equalisation by optimisation, has largely disappeared and with it the valued behaviour dictated by the group. What was once seen as a social taboo is now unleashed. The idea of being ashamed of our deviant behaviour will largely disappear. The corrective effect of the group on the individual thus stops to exist.

In this new situation the 'old-fashioned' romantic thoughts also disappear. Who could this girl be sitting opposite from you on the train? And where is she going to? These questions are now simply answered, as she is discussing her whole life's history on her mobile phone, speaking loud enough for all to hear. This gained freedom can, of course, be seen as a liberation. It seems apparent to see an advantage in the individual becoming unchained by the group. But if the corrective behaviour accompanying shame disappears, so will the behaviour disappear belonging to its antagonist, namely the meaning of being proud of something.

How will individuals find acknowledgement and attach value to matters, when society has reached phase 3, that of communication? When the taboos from phase 2 have disappeared, when society is economically largely levelled out, when individuals are of a post-war generation (who haven't helped build up the society they are in), and when placing our own imprint on society becomes pressured, then, by following the path of least resistance, the next step would be exploring the boundaries of the present phase. In doing so, the world is accepted as is, however all is subsequently ridiculed. The consequence is that nothing is sacred anymore, as our behaviour is no longer answerable to group etiquette. The countless movies on the internet of people doing ridiculous things as sillily as possible is one of many examples. As individuals attach no value to their actions and needn't feel ashamed of them, these actions deliver the shortest route to fame, to those '15 seconds of shame'. The great defect of this is obvious, since it's value has been lost. Everything is ridiculed, everything must be able to be discussed and everyone may know, or rather, everyone must know. The next question we are forced to ask is: how can we live in a society without values? Perhaps this is one reason why so many individuals of the industrialised countries have mental problems and see psychiatrists; in the end, it seems life is pretty 'worth'-less.

Prosperity

At the end of phase 2 of the social development there's still a rather rushed way of life, especially because the individual needs to manage a lot on his own, and the scarce time off seems to slip through his fingers. This is a world dominated by consumption and provoked by the media, where the expressions must be ever more stimulating, short, quick, sharp and sensational to maintain the attention of the consumer, and to seduce him into purchasing the next product. This in itself isn't strange, as the available time limits our possibilities. We can only focus our attention on one thing at a time. We read an article or answer someone's question, but reading that specific blog will have to be put off until a later moment. With the array of media-expressions present in this phase and the resulting information overload, it's no wonder that we have, and take, increasingly less time to absorb information. As a result, the information is presented even more concise in order to answer to the reader's need. It may be clear that this also leads to a shift in the appreciation. We benefit from short, clear and unambiguous answers instead of elaborate, profound background discourses. Appreciation, which can be found in silence, concentration, profundity of thought, and actual attention, there simply is no time for it.

Another influential aspect at the end of phase 2 is that the material prosperity is at its peak. In this period the average citizen has acquired such material wealth, that for the first time in history we may speak of abundance instead of scarcity for the majority of the people. The world around us is now mostly expressed in economic terms.

> Instead of forming abstract concepts where it is necessary and useful, everything, including ourselves, is being abstractified; the concrete reality of people and things to which we can relate with the reality of our own person, is replaced by abstractions, by ghosts that embody different quantities, but not different qualities. It is quite customary to talk about a "three-million-dollar bridge," a "twenty-cent cigar," a "five-dollar watch," and this not only from the standpoint of the manufacturer or the consumer in the process of buying it, but as the essential point in the description. When one speaks of the "three-million-dollar bridge," one is not primarily concerned with its usefulness or beauty, that is, with its concrete qualities, but one speaks of it as of a commodity, the main quality of which is its exchange value, expressed in a quantity, that of money.[47]

In this phase the individual no longer knows what to buy for his money, and in this abundance lies the beginning of decadence. These days we are bored easier, and disinterested quicker by our newest purchases. When a child is overwhelmed with toys and sweets, then the abundance of it nullifies the effect of the surprise of receiving something new and/or exceptional. Consequentially, the toys and sweets on the whole devaluate in meaning.

This is a period in which more possessions don't automatically contribute to our becoming happier. Prosperity in the industrialised societies has risen greatly after the Second World War. However, studies of the last few decades have shown that the number of happy people has remained the same in this period.[48] Apparently, from a certain point in time, the accumulation of more wealth no longer matters; we don't become happier owning a third car or a fourth television set. This would mean that there's a certain limit, and, when we cross it, our happiness or well-being actually no longer increases. In the absolute sense we can forever gain more wealth, and even be more content with it. But, beyond this limit the accumulation of wealth is no longer relevant to how we *experience* this wealth, as we no longer experience that we become happier proportionately.

> There's a clear counter balance between the effects of income on the experience of wellbeing and on life satisfaction. Higher income brings forth greater satisfaction, far beyond the point where it has any effect on the experience of wellbeing.[49]

Initially, not everyone profits from this increase in wealth. When in the second half of the 19th century the industrial revolution really set off, the number of suicides in France, for instance, increased with 355%.[50] And in Hungary, during the period between 1970 and 1990, welfare grew by 300%, while the number of deaths increased with 20%.[51] So in the beginning the advantages of the new economic situation are reserved for a few individuals, and the majority of citizens is unable to pick its fruits yet. But, when the society develops further, and the differences in income keep decreasing, then, at the end of phase 2 there will be a tipping point, after which the whole population will be able to enter into phase 3.

> So whether we look at health, happiness or other measures of wellbeing there is a consistent picture. In poorer countries, economic development continues to be very important for human wellbeing. Increases in their material living standards result in substantial improvements both in objective measures of wellbeing like life expectancy, and in subjective ones like happiness. But as nations join the ranks of the affluent developed countries, further rises in income count for less and less.[52]

Toward the end of phase 2 of the social development it is among others the status anxiety that makes us go beyond the limits of our sense of well-being. This no longer produces a useful outcome, other than the probability of an eventual burn-out. In phase 3, other standards and values apply, and a different attitude is required, which sets new standards for our well-being.

> Civic sense, social equality, and control over our own lives increase well-being, because they diminish the stress that people are other-

wise vulnerable to when they live together. At the same time, they increase our freedom to shape our lives according to our talents and opportunities.[53]

In a society that finds itself in the third, communicative, phase, the value of material goods is given a different meaning than it had in a society in phase 2. While, in a technocracy, more and more goods, such as music, films, books, or text in general, are digitised or are digital by nature, such as websites and emails, the character of the value given to these articles also changes. We no longer visit the local shop to buy a record or an audio CD because it has a nice cover, and we no longer return home with the physical object to show it to our friends and listen to it together. Instead, we download one specific title that we like, and the only thing showing up for it is an image of the cover on our small mobile music player. Digital products with information stored on them become more and more important in this phase. Now it's not about having a bookcase filled with books, or owning an extensive film collection. It's more about having access to these data. The subscriptions of internet providers are based on this idea. We pay a fixed rate per month, which gives us access to the internet. The number of websites or documents we look at or download is no longer important.

The traditional retail channels dramatically change in phase 3 as the classic economic model of phase 2, which ranges from whole seller to retailer, and from trading in physical goods to business and/or client services, is transformed in the digital age. Travel agencies, music stores, the local kiosk, and eventually the bookstores, have much to suffer from it. The large online retailers and the mail-order companies will especially see an increase in sales. In phase 3 we book our flight online, hotel included, we order music, films and (e-)books online, only because the collection of the online stores greatly exceeds that of the traditional metropolitan bookstores. We download a game and check out the quickest route from A to B on our mobile phone or navigation system. The book, the CD, the DVD, the map, the travel ticket, the magazine, these are all products that until recently had unique physical appearances. In time these will dramatically decrease in numbers and will largely be replaced by their digital equivalents. With this, the appreciation value of the products changes. The smell of a book, the cover of that latest CD and accompanying booklet, the travel ticket, which we lay ready a few days before travelling and the holiday feeling that it already provokes, the map that we carried in our hands while we stood on the mountain top after a long walk, these are all unique objects, embodying the emotional effects of a certain moment in time. These will be replaced by a bar code or data that automatically disappears from our mobile phone as soon as we pass the entrance. The transition from the analogue to the digital phase is a step into a less tangible world.

This phase in the social development process is already visible, because the changes are happening now in large parts of the industrialised societies. The fact that the access to digital information is gaining social and economic importance, becomes clear when the internet connection fails, the company employees' activities abruptly stop, and the company processes largely grind to a halt. This illustrates our dependence on the digital world in our present business and personal spheres. Generally, the older we get the more we tend to become attached to the old ways, to fixed values which we've seen changing and disappearing as time passes. At certain moments in time, we look back at our personal histories with a somewhat coloured, nostalgic, view. Actually, every day there are minute changes taking place in the individual sphere, which will slowly bring society as a whole to its next developmental phase.

The last phase

Has everything then become 'worthless' in this last phase of the social development? Do our youths have a worthless future ahead of them? Have all the tangible products become insensitive digital carriers? Have the emotions, such as shame and romantics, completely gone? No, certainly not.

Especially in this phase, many positive changes in society occur, in which the individual enters a new, unique situation. There are more people who want to express themselves. And they are given all the necessary space to share their creations with everyone, as the possibilities to share them in the (digital) world are unprecedented. The personal acknowledgement of these creations by others and the value we attach to our own creations increase. The self-confidence is greater than ever before. Not only does the individual feel more conscious of himself and sees the consequences of his actions, more ethical consciousness arises between societies as well, a consequence of globalisation and permanent connections between individuals all over the world.

In phase 2 of the social development the prime motivation for manufacturers was to gain maximum profit, and for the consumer the hunger for whatever the market had to offer. What applies to both is an aim for pride and value, and a strive for acknowledgement by others. When we sell many products as manufacturers, we show that our company is doing well, that we're successful. When, as a consumer, we've just bought the latest product, and we show it to our friends, we show that we participate, that we belong to the group, thus we gain acknowledgement.

In phase 3 this acknowledgement becomes even more important. The manufacturer must produce a product in a universally fair manner: the environment must not be harmed, various safety regulations must be complied with, crops may not be sprayed with suspicious aids, animals must be kept in the best possible circumstances when intended for consumption, and the company must at best be socially involved by sponsoring charities. To keep their image up in this phase, companies must show socially justified entrepreneurship. The Non-Governmental Organisations (NGO's) play an even greater role in voicing the concerns of specific groups of society. These NGO's operate internationally. So, the attention for the new concerns rapidly spreads beyond national borders, especially since the globalisation has become highly advanced in this phase. The impact of the NGO's even increases when we take into account that individuals now let their identity or status depend less on a nation or country. The political system that suits this situation best is a technocracy. This is a government which policies are guided by scientific facts, which acts on the basis of ethical consciousness for the good of its people, and is less coloured by a political trend or party. Subsequently in the second part of phase 3, there's much more room for individual development. There's room for silence, concentration, absorption, and real attention. It's difficult to predict how and when this phase will really establish itself, actually it's just as difficult as it was for the people living in phase 1 of the social development to grasp the idea of living in phase 2. In this third phase the differences in gender, income, skin colour, and various other characteristics of the phases 1 and 2 of the social development lose their importance. The new generation, which is now growing up with the internet and all sorts of other communicative possibilities, is judged by the present generation, which mostly bases itself on the behavioural rules from phase 2 of the social development. But, we can't judge too fast or hard here, as we are yet on the brink of many new developments. Whether these new technological means provide better communication between individuals, or whether we become completely dependent on it, all this lies in the future. It is clear, however, that the possibilities for constant communication have a far reaching influence on our daily lives, these will increase in the future. It is clear as well, that in this phase of human history there's never been a chance yet for so many people to develop themselves in all kinds of areas. Never before have so many people been able to gain access to so much knowledge. In phase 1 the information is but reserved for a number of people at the top of the hierarchy. In phase 3, however, everyone has access to (practically) all information at any given moment. This is a fantastic provision for the creative, self-realising individual. So this last phase is one in which every individual can fully develop himself, and where all the possibilities are present to strive for self-knowledge, insight and self-control.

New questions also accompany this new phase. In a society based on technocracy, tensions will arise between the requirements and duties society demands or imposes on its citizens, and the acquired individual freedom, a basis for full individual development. On the one hand the question arises whether the individual has the idea of 'being at home' within the given society. Can an individual completely fulfil his development? Are there limits that confine him? On the other hand we find society. What does it 'demand' of its citizens? Which freedoms can the society guarantee? It eventually amounts to the trust the government has in the individual, and vice versa. If this trust is strongly tested, when for example the individual freedom becomes too great a threat for the government, a police state can emerge, where the government will use all the technological means available to confine this individual freedom. So, in tomorrows technocratic society the preservation of individual freedom will become ever more apparent. The great 'danger' is that the technological developments will go faster, than the time needed for individual self-realisation. Albert Einstein thought we already made that step arguing: 'It has become appallingly obvious that our technology has exceeded our humanity.' When this actually happens, then technology will 'win', while the social development, in the rules of communication, ethics, laws, and specifically the individuals being part of it, will go much slower. At a certain moment we will be faced with the greater effects of the technological developments, and then perhaps there's no way back, probably because we've already become so dependent on them. What follows is the adaptation of culture, rules of communication, ethics, laws, etc., although when positioning man at the centre these aspects should play a decisive role. Will we take a pill to live as long as possible because we still want to do so many things, and do we only take it because it will be possible in the near future? If we ask this question first, when technology hasn't progressed that far yet, we can make an evaluation based on our greater self-reflection, our values and virtues, etc. Then we might not take that pill, because we think life should be ending, because we want to weigh things to their value, and we would feel that technology mustn't outrun us. In any case, we will then be able to make an informed decision about whether we want to take that pill deliberately or take it without thinking about the consequences.

6.5 The Reward

We began this part by stating that man has a conscience, and that, by reflecting on his own situation, he can understand that a time will come when The One Self seizes to exist. Not only does this *sound* harsh, it *is* harsh. Thus said, it is rather difficult to deny that this comes as a real negative 'reward', even though the disappearance of The One Self lies at the core of every human being. Humans are conscious, right-minded individuals who flee into the behaviourisms of a neurotic type to keep off the terrible reality as long as possible, which irrevocably lies waiting for them. Just because we have a physical body, this doesn't mean that we're merely animals. And just because we have certain mental capacity, it doesn't mean we can ascend gods throne. It's this ambiguity, this dualism that makes us unique as a human species. This continuous flux between antagonists gives us a playing field in which we experience greater and lesser moments in our lives.

The struggle between our natural origin and our mental capacities is described in a poem by Alexander Pope:[54]

> Know, then, thyself, presume not God to scan;
> The proper study of mankind is man.
> Placed on this isthmus of a middle state,
> A being darkly wise, and rudely great:
> With too much knowledge for the sceptic side,
> With too much weakness for the stoic's pride,
> He hangs between; in doubt to act, or rest;
> In doubt to deem himself a god, or beast;
> In doubt his mind or body to prefer;
> Born but to die, and reasoning but to err;
> Alike in ignorance, his reason such,
> Whether he thinks too little, or too much:
> Chaos of thought and passion, all confused;
> Still by himself abused, or disabused;
> Created half to rise, and half to fall;
> Great lord of all things, yet a prey to all;
> Sole judge of truth, in endless error hurled:
> The glory, jest, and riddle of the world!

Gradually we've uncovered the processes and motivations lying hidden behind our daily worries. We've shed a light on life, which is veiled by each neurotic type. The harsh observation of the inevitability of death claims a moment of reflection for each of us to perhaps gain a different look on life. For, beside death as an objective biological process, there is a subjective infill every individual makes of life, of the time before and after his death. For instance, by acting in a respectful and peaceful manner, we can lay a foundation for a purposeful life. We can develop the insight, that although during our life both good fortune and misery will cross our path, this realisation is what makes us human. By developing self-control, self-knowledge and insight a balance can be established, where the two antagonists power and fear, lying closest to our core, are ruled out. This can eventually lead to the self-realisation of the individual.

There are some days, when it is neither hot nor cold, when we can put on a coat and leave it off just as well, when the trees don't move but we still sense a light breeze on our face, when we're untroubled and have nothing on our mind, when it doesn't matter what we've done before or what will happen next. At these moments the antagonists are balanced and they've cancelled each other out. This is a feeling of utter tranquility, of complete balance. This inner peace, this balanced state is neither a slackening, nor a folly, but rather a state of complete control over the moment, over our own lives. This self-control provides us insight into human functioning. It reminds us of the Greek proverb 'know thyself'. At the end of phase 3 it is no longer necessary for the individual to extend control, as was necessary previously for a society in phase 1 and 2 of its development. It is important for each of us to achieve this balance ourselves, as it lies at the heart of individual self-realisation. For, when it goes undiscovered by the individuals themselves other forces will come in to action, as Foley describes:

> Those who do not produce their own solution must be using some-
> one else's. As Nietzsche warned: 'he who cannot obey himself will
> be commanded'. Worse, the someone else who commands is likely
> to be the average contemporary, and the solution a weak mixture of
> contemporary recommendations and anathemas.[55]

If we have no control of ourselves, nor possess or use any measure of knowledge, insight or self-reflection, then it will be filled in for us by someone else. At such a moment others have power over us on the specific subject or situation, and we stop being the completely autonomous individual we otherwise would have been. This control, this power, is important. The more we influence our own lives (e.g. by the type of work we do) and our environment (e.g. our position within society), the better this is for us. If we lack control, then the chances are that we will be faced with stress at any given moment. Employees in lower functions live shorter, they have less control over their working circumstances and are dependent on what their superiors decide for them. But, the reverse is true as well: senior citizens in an elderly home, who are given more to say about their daily schedule, are less ill, happier and live longer.[56]

Along with the most basic aspects of self-preservation, such as food and reproduction, Fromm describes the fully mentally healthy, developed human being:

> The need for relatedness, transcendence, rootedness, the need for a
> sense of identity and the need for a frame of orientation and devotion.
> The great passions of man, his lust for power, his vanity, his search
> for truth, his passion for love and brotherliness, his destructiveness as
> well as his creativeness, every powerful desire which motivates man's
> actions, is rooted in this specific human source.[57]

The next citation of Fromm also describes the completely developed human being, embracing the deficiencies inherent to human existence:

> The aim of life is to live it intensely, to be fully born, to be fully awake.
> To emerge from the ideas of infantile grandiosity into the conviction
> of one's real though limited strength; to be able to accept the paradox
> that every one of us is the most important thing there is in the uni-
> verse–and at the same time not more important than a fly or a blade of
> grass. To be able to love life, and yet to accept death without terror; to
> tolerate uncertainty about the most important questions with which
> life confronts us–and yet to have faith in our thought and feeling,
> inasmuch as they are truly ours.[58]

We also find an ancient description of the completely developed human being in Nietzsche's work, exemplifying Goethe, as Bishop writes:

> Nietzsche embraces the Pindaric imperative—"we, however, want to
> *become who we are*"—which means a commitment to becoming "human
> beings who are new, unique, incomparable, who give themselves laws,
> who create themselves!". And there is [...] a model for this Pindaric
> self: as an ideal of "giving style to one's character," Nietzsche suggests

we turn to Goethe. In *Twilight of the Idols*, Goethe is presented as "a spirit become free," who "dares to allow himself the whole compass and wealth of naturalness, who is strong enough for this freedom," and who "stands in the midst of the universe with a joyful and trusting fatalism."[...] And Nietzsche's examples of the things for which it is worth living on the earth—"virtue, art, music, dance, reason, intellect"—or, in other words, "something transfiguring, subtle, mad, and divine"— are embodied in "the admired wholeness" of someone like Goethe, in the embrace of "reason, sensuality, feeling, will".[59]

So far we've looked at the complete development of the individual, at self-realisation. This development has the best chance of success when it takes place in a society where individuals can fully develop themselves, where the society gives the individual that much freedom and doesn't impose upon them limiting rules that slow down their self-realisation. This is a society in which individuals have the space to develop and express themselves creatively, to be critical of others and especially of themselves, so that they can come to new insights by self-reflection.

How do we achieve this situation? How can people individually, but also a society as a whole, strive for this advanced state of development?

It is tricky to answer for a society as a whole, as there's an array of aspects and influences to deal with, and it becomes even more difficult to predict when this could take place. If we take the society as a group of individuals, we can make certain statements. When we look at phase 2 of the social development, and especially at the neurotic type 2, then it must be most difficult for this group to take that step towards phase 3. For, how can this neurotic type, who, consciously or not, attunes himself to group behaviour and wallows in the wealths of prosperity, evolve to a fully autonomous individual, who receives appreciation and acknowledgement from his surroundings for the specific qualities he has developed? Or, as Elster put it:

> 'Those governed by the reality principle seek accurate beliefs, whereas those subject to the pleasure principle seek pleasant beliefs.'[60]

Although initially approaching phase 3 seems like a big step, there are a number of factors that we've come across before, which will show their forces again.

One important factor dominating the way of life of the neurotic type 2 is group behaviour. This behaviour can be steered externally, for instance by a clear message or by economic factors. When certain behaviour is at some time forbidden by the government, or when the consumer has to pay more and more for certain products, then this group will gradually adapt its behaviour. For instance, from a certain moment it was made compulsory by law to wear a seatbelt in the car. These campaigns sometimes go on for a decade, especially when a large group must be reached, and because it must bring about behavioural change to all car drivers. With a fine as a big stick, just about everyone now 'automatically' uses the seatbelt. But, there are also more subtle compulsory forms, such as, for instance, the trends to a healthy diet, to more physical activity, which rather focus on achieving health ideals and a more conscious way of living without the use of direct sanctions. As is often the case with group behaviour, in the beginning there are a number of trendsetters, the large group will follow later.

There's another important factor in phase 3 of the social development, and that is status. In phase 2 status is mostly focussed on material or social matters, but in phase 3 status will be measured by the individual himself, on his erudition, his knowledge, his insight and his composure. The status is still determined by the hero. He sets the framework, after which the individual provides the infill. As we've seen, this behaviour of the hero already starts in the natural phase 1: by inflicting physical damage with brute force, his power is established or strengthened. In phase 2 status is achieved in a 'social' manner, by gaining power in an economic, social or scientific area. And, in phase 3 we derive status from our goodness, artistry, wisdom, conscious deeds or by following up on established forms of common decency.[61] As time passes, the differences between groups of people or individuals within phases 1 and 2 become less prominent, resulting in phase 3 in individuals who can distinguish themselves, maximally develop themselves, and who are completely accepted by their surroundings. The circumstances might change in the different phases, but the underlying mechanisms remain the same.

However at a societal level, it still is a great step to evolve from phase 2 to phase 3, and at an individual level to transform from the type 2 neurotic to the type 3 neurotic. But, if we don't come to this insight on our own, we will be forced by the circumstances that actually change. Looking back in time, we can also state that the people that lived 1000 years ago couldn't suspect how we live today, for example not governed by a dictatorship, in a much evolved social society, and with large scale production, instead of living off a small patch of land on which only a limited amount of crops can grow. The advancements in economy, political influence, civil guarantees by laws, social provisions, the increase in personal possessions and the general living standard, to name but a few, have changed immensely in the last centuries. As is clear from this list, we must bear in mind that we can't concentrate on just one of these aspects. The human development within society evolves along all facets of life, as described in part two, i.e. politically, economically, socially and religiously. Fromm describes the simultaneous development of these different 'spheres':

> Man is a unit; his thinking, feeling, and his practice of life are insepa-rably connected. He cannot be free in his thought when he is not free emotionally; and he cannot be free emotionally if he is dependent and unfree in his practice of life, in his economic and social relations. Trying to advance radically in one sector to the exclusion of others must necessarily lead to the result to which it did lead, namely, that the radical demands in one sphere are fulfilled only by a few individuals, while for the majority they become formulae and rituals, serving to cover up the fact that in other spheres nothing has changed. Undoubt-edly *one* step of integrated progress in all spheres of life will have more far-reaching and more lasting results for the progress of the human race than a hundred steps preached -and even for a short while lived-in only one isolated sphere. Several thousands of years of failure in 'isolated progress' should be a rather convincing lesson.[62]

Knowing that the development must take place in all these spheres, provides us with a foothold on our way to a society, which is 'healthy' and where the citizens are most happy. This is obviously not a simple task. For most of us, at this moment in human history, it's not within hands' reach, but rather miles away. And, for the individual living in miserable circumstances, searching for food and drink every day, the struggle for survival has a much higher priority. For now, we can only guess as to when the conditions will be optimal for the process of self-realisation to actually take place on a large scale. However, mankind will eventually strive for self-realisation. Man will always be an inquisitive being. It applies to all of us that, by the knowledge we gain now and by concatenating our future experiences, we will be more conscious of the short time we spend on earth. At this time, we need life to understand death, and we need death to appreciate life.

References

Part 1 – Eternity

1 Foley, M. *The Age of Absurdity: Why Modern Life makes it Hard to be Happy.* London : Simon & Schuster, 2011, p. 63 (as cited in Schopenhauer, 1974).

2 http://en.wikiquote.org/wiki/Cicero

3 Johansen, K. F. *A History of Ancient Philosophy: From the Beginnings to Augustine.* Taylor & Francis e-Library, 2005, p. 69.

4 Kahneman, D. *Thinking, Fast and Slow.* London : Penguin Books, 2012, p. 90.

5 Fukuyama, F. *The End of History and the Last Man.* New York : Free Press, 2006, p. 155.

6 Rousseau, J. J. *The Social Contract, or Principles of Political Right.* 1782. http://www.constitution.org/jjr/socon.htm.

7 Stokes, P. *Philosophy: 100 Essential Thinkers.* London : Arcturus, 2002, p. 99.

8 Fromm, E. *Escape from Freedom.* New York : Rinehart & Co, 1941, p. 139.

9 *Ibid.* 4, p. 301.

10 Becker, E. *The Denial of Death.* New York : Free Press Paperback, 1997, p. 52 (as cited in Maslow, 1963).

11 Klein, S. *The Science of Happiness: How Our Brains Make Us Happy – and What We Can Do to Get Happier.* Cambridge : Da Capo Press, 2006, p. 12-15.

12 Wiseman, R. *Paranormality: Why We See What Isn't There.* London : Macmillan, 2011, p. 25-26.

13 *Ibid.* 11, p. 185.

14 *Ibid.* 4, p. 430.

15 Elster, J. *Explaining Social Behavior: More Nuts and Bolts for the Social Sciences.* New York : Cambridge University Press, 2007, p. 71.

16 Lamme, V. *De vrije wil bestaat niet: Over wie er echt de baas is in het brein.* Amsterdam : Bert Bakker, 2010, p. 58.

17 Duhigg, Ch. *The Power of Habit: Why We Do What We Do and How to Change.* London : Random House Books, 2013, p. 225.

18 *Ibid.* 17, p. 92-93.

19 *Ibid.* 15, p. 210.

20 Hamlyn, D. W. *A History of Western Philosophy*. London : Penguin Books, 1988, p. 19.

21 *Ibid*. 7, p. 15.

22 Adkinson, R. (Ed.). *Sacred Symbols: A Visual Tour of World Faith*. London : Thames & Hudson, 2009, p. 424.

23 Wilkinson, P. *Eyewitness Companions: Religions*. London : Dorling Kindersley Ltd, 2008, p. 178.

24 *Ibid*. 22, p. 562.

25 *Ibid*. 22, p. 364.

26 *Ibid*. 22, p. 424.

27 *Ibid*. 7, p. 27.

28 http://www.insidescience.org/content/first-detailed-photos-atoms/1184

29 Armstrong, K. *A History of God: The 4,000-Year Quest of Judaism, Christianity and Islam*. New York : Alfred A. Knopf, 1994, p. 343 (as cited in Jourdain, 1966).

30 http://wiki.answers.com/Q/How_much_better_can_a_dog_smell_than_a_human

31 Hawking, S. *A Brief History of Time*. Bantam Press : London, 1998, p. 46-47.

32 *Ibid*. 29, p. 298 (as cited in Krailsheimer, 1966).

Part 2 – World

1 Fukuyama, F. *The End of History and the Last Man*. New York : Free Press, 2006, p. 153-161.

2 Cornelis, A. *Logica van het gevoel: Filosofie van de Stabiliteitslagen in de Cultuur als Nesteling der Emoties*. Amsterdam : Stichting Essence, 1998, p. 2, 217, 617.

3 Fromm, E. *The Sane Society*. London : Routledge, 2008, p. 242 (as cited in Fourier, 1851).

4 Watson, P. *Ideas: A History of Thought and Invention, from Fire to Freud*. New York : Harper Perennial, 2006, p. 643.

5 *Ibid*. 1, p. 60.

6 O'Neil, D. Early Modern Homo sapiens. 1999-2013. http://anthro.palomar.edu/homo2/mod_homo_4.htm.

7 Swaab, D. *We Are Our Brains: From the Womb to Alzheimer's*. London : Allen Lane, 2014, p. 277.

8 *Ibid*. 4, p. 28.

9 http://www.youtube.com/watch?v=Hqp6GnYqIjQ

10 http://www.prisonexp.org.

11 *Ibid*. 4, p. 53.

12 Santon, K. (Ed.), McKay, L. (Ed.). *Atlas of World History*. Bath : Parragon, 2005. p. 11.

13 *Ibid.* 12, p. 17.

14 Le Goff, J. *Medieval Civilization 400 – 1500.* Oxford : Basil Blackwell Ltd, 1988, p. 74.

15 *Ibid.* 4, p. 664-665.

16 *Ibid.* 14, p. 255.

17 *Ibid.* 14, p. 54.

18 *Ibid.* 14, p. 316.

19 *Ibid.* 14, p. 292-293.

20 *Ibid.* 14, p. 261.

21 Rousseau, J. J. *A Discourse upon the Origin and the Foundation of the Inequality among Mankind.* 1755. http://www.gutenberg.org/ebooks/11136.

22 *Ibid.* 1, p. xvii-xviii.

23 *Ibid.* 4, p. 541 (as cited in Buchan, 2003).

24 *Ibid.* 1, p. 294.

25 Fromm, E. *Escape from Freedom.* New York : Rinehart & Co, 1941, p. 242-243.

26 *Ibid.* 25, p. 243-244.

27 *Ibid.* 1, p. xiv-xv.

28 Botton, A. de. *Status Anxiety.* London : Penguin books, 2005, p. 277-303.

29 *Ibid.* 4, p. 603-611.

30 Rousseau, J. J. *The Social Contract, or Principles of Political Right.* 1782. http://www.constitution.org/jjr/socon.htm.

31 *Ibid.* 4, p. 705 (as cited in Chadwick, 1975/1985).

32 *Ibid.* 4, p. 499.

33 *Ibid.* 1, p. 49-50 (as cited in Doyle, 1983).

34 *Ibid.* 3, p. 105.

35 Law, S. *Eyewitness Companions: Philosophy.* London : Dorling Kindersley Ltd, 2007, p. 162-164.

36 Wilkinson, P. *Eyewitness Companions: Religions.* London : Dorling Kindersley Ltd, 2008, p. 292

37 Stokes, P. *Philosophy: 100 Essential Thinkers.* London : Arcturus, 2002, p. 13.

38 *Ibid.* 4, p. 61.

39 Armstrong, K. *A History of God: The 4,000-Year Quest of Judaism, Christianity and Islam.* New York : Alfred A. Knopf, 1994, p. 27.

40 *Ibid.* 4, p. 107.

41 *Ibid.* 36, p. 16.

42 *Ibid.* 4, p. 376.

43 *Ibid.* 4, p. 334.

44 *Ibid.* 1, p. 216.

45 *Ibid.* 4, p. 325-326.

46 *Ibid.* 4, p. 475.

47 *Ibid.* 7, p. 246-247.

48 *Ibid.* 14, p. 75.

49 Botton, A. de. *The Pleasures and Sorrows of Work.* London : Penguin Books, 2010, p. 76-78.

50 Duhigg, Ch. *The Power of Habit: Why We Do What We Do and How to Change.* London : Random House Books, 2013, p. 185-191.

51 *Ibid.* 3, p. 177.

52 http://en.wikipedia.org/wiki/McDonaldisation.

53 *Ibid.* 3, p. 159-160.

54 *Ibid.* 25, p. 102-103.

55 Klein, S. *The Science of Happiness: How Our Brains Make Us Happy – and What We Can Do to Get Happier.* Cambridge : Da Capo Press, 2006, p. 239.

56 Wilkinson, R., Pickett, K. *The Spirit Level: Why Equality is Better for Everyone.* London : Penguin Group, 2010, p. 10.

57 *Ibid.* 25, p. 91.

58 *Ibid.* 4, p. 398.

59 *Ibid.* 4, p. 607.

60 *Ibid.* 1, p. 290.

61 *Ibid.* 56, p. 7.

62 *Ibid.* 56, p. 9.

63 Helliwell, J., Layard, R., Sachs, J. (Ed.). *World Happiness Report 2013.* New York : UN SDSN, 2013. http://unsdsn.org/happiness/

64 http://www.guardian.co.uk/technology/2009/oct/14/finland-broadband

65 *Ibid.* 4, p. 654.

66 Riemen, R. *Nobility of Spirit: A Forgotten Ideal.* London : Yale University Press, 2008, p. 68.

67 *Ibid.* 1, p. 126.

68 http://en.wikipedia.org/wiki/Ancient_Egypt

69 *Ibid.* 21.

70 *Ibid.* 56, p. 267-268.

71 *Ibid.* 56, p. 20.

72 *Ibid.* 1, p. 276.

73 *Ibid.* 35, p. 82.

74 *Ibid.* 35, p. 297.

75 *Ibid.* 4, p. 739.

76 Voltaire. *Épître à l'Auteur du Livre des Trois Imposteurs.* 1770. See also: http://www.whitman.edu/VSA/trois.imposteurs.html

77 Gould, S. J. *Rocks of Ages: Science and Religion in the Fullness of Life.* The Ballantine Publishing Group : New York, 1999, p. 94.

78 Münchhausen Trilemma. See also: http://rationalwiki.org/wiki/M%C3%BCnchhausen_Trilemma

79 *Ibid.* 3, p. 138.

80 http://en.wikipedia.org/wiki/15_minutes_of_fame

81 *Ibid.* 49, p. 35.

82 Klein, S. *The Science of Happiness: How Our Brains Make Us Happy – and What We Can Do to Get Happier.* Cambridge : Da Capo Press, 2006, p. 152.

83 *Ibid.* 3, p. 168.

84 *Ibid.* 37, p. 191.

Part 3 – Man

1 Hamlyn, D. W. *A History of Western Philosophy.* London : Penguin Books, 1988.

2 Hofstadter, D. R., Dennett, D. C. *The Mind's I: Fantasies and Reflections on Self and Soul.* New York : Basic Books, 1981.

3 Jones, S. *Darwin's Island: The Galapagos in the Garden of England.* London : Little, Brown, 2009, p. 163-185.

4 Fromm, E. *Escape from Freedom.* New York : Rinehart & Co, 1941, p. 17.

5 Becker, E. *The Denial of Death.* New York : Free Press Paperback, 1997, p. 87.

6 Savater, F. *Lof der Godloosheid: Kleine filosofie van ongeloof en twijfel.* Utrecht : Bijleveld, 2010, p. 113-114 (as cited in Blumenberg, 1979).

7 *Ibid.* 5, p. 5.

8 *Ibid.* 4, p. 103-104.

9 Fromm, E. *The Sane Society.* London : Routledge, 2008, p. 27-28.

10 *Ibid.* 5, p. 16 (as cited in Zilboorg, 1943).

11 *Ibid.* 5, p. 17 (as cited in Zilboorg, 1943).

12 *Ibid.* 4, p. 118-119.

13 *Ibid.* 5, p. 264 (as cited in Marcuse, 1962).

14 *Ibid.* 5, p. 177-178.

15 *Ibid.* 5, p. 78.

16 Botton, A. de. *Status Anxiety.* London : Penguin books, 2005, p. 207.

17 *Ibid.* 5, p. 3.

18 Ingersoll, R. G. *The Works of Robert G. Ingersoll.* New York : The Dresden Publishing Co., C.P. Farrell, Vol. 6, 1902. http://www.gutenberg.org/ebooks/38806.

19 Savater, F. *Lof der Godloosheid: Kleine filosofie van ongeloof en twijfel.* Utrecht : Bijleveld, 2010, p. 13.

20 *Ibid.* 9, p. 22-23.

21 Lamme, V. *De vrije wil bestaat niet: Over wie er echt de baas is in het brein.* Amsterdam : Bert Bakker, 2010, p. 208. See also: http://science.nasa.gov/ science-news/science-at-nasa/2001/ast24may_1/

22 Swaab, D. *We Are Our Brains: From the Womb to Alzheimer's.* London : Allen Lane, 2014, p. 27.

23 *Ibid.* 22, p. 174.

24 *Ibid.* 21, p. 144 (as cited in Bouchard, 2004).

25 *Ibid.* 22, p. 256-260.

26 Kahneman, D. *Thinking, Fast and Slow.* London : Penguin Books, 2012, p. 35.

27 Klein, S. *The Science of Happiness: How Our Brains Make Us Happy – and What We Can Do to Get Happier.* Cambridge : Da Capo Press, 2006, p. 58.

28 *Ibid.* 5, p. 160.

29 *Ibid.* 5, p. 166.

30 Botton, A. de. *The Pleasures and Sorrows of Work.* London : Penguin Books, 2010, p. 116.

31 *Ibid.* 9, p. 119-120.

32 Goldacre, B. *Bad Science: Quacks, Hacks, and Big Pharma Flacks.* New York : Faber and Faber, 2010, p. 182-183.

33 http://www.youtube.com/watch?v=OSsPfbup0ac

34 *Ibid.* 16, p. 3-4.

35 Wiseman, R. *Paranormality: Why We See What Isn't There.* London : Macmillan, 2011, p. 86.

36 Wilkinson, R., Pickett, K. *The Spirit Level: Why Equality is Better for Everyone.* London : Penguin Group, 2010, p. 230.

37 *Ibid.* 36, p. 9.

38 *Ibid.* 36, p. 228-229.

39 Foley, M. *The Age of Absurdity: Why Modern Life makes it Hard to be Happy.* London : Simon & Schuster, 2011, p. 36.

40 *Ibid.* 5, p. 171.

41 *Ibid.* 27, p. 43.

42 *Ibid.* 4, p. 157-175.

43 *Ibid.* 35, p. 59 (as cited in Gabbard & Twemlow, 1984).

44 Duhigg, Ch. *The Power of Habit: Why We Do What We Do and How to Change.* London : Random House Books, 2013, p. 192.

45 Fukuyama, F. *The End of History and the Last Man.* New York : Free Press, 2006, p. 174 (as cited in Smith, 1982).

46 *Ibid.* 45, p. 292.

47 *Ibid.* 9, p. 111.

48 *Ibid.* 27, p. 237.

49 *Ibid.* 36, p. 397.

50 *Ibid.* 9, p. 146.

51 *Ibid.* 27, p. 240-241.

52 *Ibid.* 36, p. 8.

53 *Ibid.* 27, p. 253.

54 Pope, A. *An Essay on Man: Epistle II*, 1734. http://www.gutenberg.org/ebooks/2428

55 *Ibid.* 39, p. 8.

56 *Ibid.* 27, p. 248-252.

57 *Ibid.* 9, p. 65-66.

58 *Ibid.* 9, p. 197.

59 Bishop, P. http://www.nietzschecircle.com/review25.html. Review of: Janaway, Chr. *Beyond Selflessness: Reading Nietzsche's Genealogy*. New York : Oxford University Press Inc., 2007.

60 Elster, J. *Explaining Social Behavior: More Nuts and Bolts for the Social Sciences*. New York : Cambridge University Press, 2007, p. 137.

61 *Ibid.* 16, p. 190-191.

62 *Ibid.* 9, p. 265-266.